LEADING MEN

LEADING MEN

TEXT BY JULIE WELCH
DESIGN BY LOUISE BRODY

FOREWORD BY JANE RUSSELL

PHOTOGRAPHS FROM
THE KOBAL COLLECTION

CONRAN OCTOPUS

First published in 1985 by
Conran Octopus Limited
37 Shelton Street
London WC2H 9HN

Text copyright © Julie Welch 1985
Layout and picture selection copyright © Louise Brody and The Kobal Collection Limited 1985

Reprinted 1990

I would like to express by heartfelt gratitude to Simon Crocker, without whose help, encouragement and advice this book would never have been produced. To Dave Kent I am deeply indebted for his invaluable advice and support and for his immense contribution to the picture research and editing. I extend my thanks to everyone at The Kobal Collection and Conran Octopus who made this book possible, especially Alex Lascelles, whose advice and understanding have been much appreciated. Many, many happy hours have been spent compiling this selection from the marvellous photographs of John Kobal's collection. I hope it gives its readers as much pleasure as it has given me in designing it. Louise Brody

Acknowledgments The publishers would like to thank the following film distribution and production companies whose film stills and publicity portraits appear in this book: Allied Artists, Anglo Amalgamated, Avco Embassy, CBS Theatrical Films, Cocinor, Columbia Pictures, Constantin, EMI, Eon, Europa Film, Juno Film, London Films, Long Road, Lucasfilm, Malpaso, MGM, Mirisch, Mutual, Orion, Paramount Pictures, Produzione Europee Associates, Rank Organisation, Rastar, Remus, Republic, RKO, Selznick Releasing Corporation, Seven Arts, Tri-Star, 20th Century-Fox, United Artists, Universal Pictures, Warner Brothers. Photographs on pages 207, 215, courtesy of Rex Features.

Edited by Vicky Hayward

Hardback ISBN 1 85029 021 0

Typeset by SX Composing Ltd
Printed and bound in Hong Kong

Frontispiece: studio portrait of Gary Cooper, c. 1930.
Foreword: studio portrait of Jane Russell, 1949.
          Photographer A.L. 'Whitey' Schaefer.

CONTENTS

FOREWORD

What would we have ever done without the beautiful fantasies brought to us by our leading men? They have made female hearts flutter and men dream heroic dreams since the beginning of the motion picture.

Any girl would have given her eye teeth to work with just one of them. You knew the leading man was going to get the lady's love, if not the lady, because, bless his heart, he had the ability to show his very soul through the lens of the camera and to make us want to put our arms around him and tell him we loved him all the way.

They came to us in assorted types as different, one from another, as can be; tall and short, rugged and tender, beautiful and, yes, even ugly. But they all had one thing in common — sex appeal combined with a quality that made them stand out in a crowd. Perhaps it is this that counts. Each is unique, yet they are all one of a kind. I do know one thing, I have never met a stupid or insensitive leading man and I have worked with quite a few — including Clark Gable, Robert Mitchum and Gilbert Roland.

Today's leading men possess similar qualities. They may not seem as beautiful to me as their predecessors, and they lack the advantage we had of the Hollywood publicity machine behind them, but they still have all the qualities we demand of leading men, especially the key one — the ability to make you interested in them and care about them.

This book of unforgettable photographs enables us all, once more, to relive our fantasies about the leading men of the movies.

INTRODUCTION

I am a fan of the movies, rather than an authority on them. I could not recount the dialogue, word for word, of *The Searchers*, or tell the story of *The Wild Bunch* down to every last detail, or, for that matter, recall the plots of every film Gary Cooper ever made. But, like everybody else, I have several favourite leading men, some of whose movies were made many years ago, others who are newcomers whose films — good, bad, or indifferent — I follow with avid interest.

There is undoubtedly a distinction between leading men and leading actors, but it is subtle and I find it difficult to pin down. A leading man's appeal is both sexual and romantic, and while sex appeal is not hard to spot, romance is elusive, captured by the moment rather than the personality or physical appeal. It may be Humphrey Bogart in the Café Americain telling Sam, 'I thought I told you never to play it', or Fred Astaire dancing cheek to cheek and spinning Ginger Rogers around and around in *Top Hat*. It could be Robert De Niro rolling in the snow with Liza Minnelli outside the judge's house in *New York, New York*, or Martine Carol undressing for Anton Walbrook as King of Bavaria, a minute after she meets him in *Lola Montes*, or the last moments of *Broadway Danny Rose*, when Woody Allen runs out into the New York street to forgive Mia Farrow.

Not long ago, I even spotted such a moment in a Clark Gable and Doris Day movie called *Teacher's Pet*. Although the film was made late in Gable's career, only two years before his death — his dimples were joined by furrows and wrinkles, his chin was jowly and the energy had gone out of his step — there was a moment in it, when Gable paused in a doorway, grabbed prim, patronizing Day and forced her into a clinch, that made it all worthwhile.

Researching this book gave me a marvellous chance to widen my knowledge of leading men to whom I had previously paid little attention, as well as to increase my perception of the importance of movies in reflecting and determining our attitudes to masculinity. I had a lot of fun looking at men in a new way, classing them according to type: the macho character like Clint Eastwood, the one who had clearly seen a lot of Bogie movies when he was growing up, and the Cary Grant smoothie. I came to realize that, although leading men will always have sexual charisma, they are never simply sex objects. They also represent masculine values and fantasies and provide the role models for their time, whether as the swashbucklers and Latin lovers of the twenties, all-American heroes of the thirties, as wisecracking private eyes of the forties, or the working-class heroes of the fifties and sixties. In modern times leading men have become more macho again. In every period, their gestures and mannerisms have been copied: Gary Cooper's drawl, Humphrey Bogart's rasping delivery, James Dean's sneer and John Wayne's swagger. And they are still imitated today.

Looking at leading men in this perspective, it is also clear that the same type re-emerges at different periods — it is simply the packaging that changes to accommodate the fashions and attitudes of the time. The swashbuckling adventure hero who first appeared in the shape of Douglas Fairbanks Sr in the twenties has returned in various forms in succeeding decades: Errol Flynn and Tyrone Power, Stewart Granger and Tony Curtis in his early years. Now, in modern times, we have Harrison Ford. Rudolph Valentino, whose sadistic, thrusting sensuality inspired women to erotic fantasy and men to envy and derision, was first in a line of Latin lovers that stretches all the way to John Travolta.

To confuse matters further, a star can be a leading man only at certain stages of his career: Spencer Tracy, for example, in the films he made with Katharine Hepburn before his persona matured into that of the Wise Old Man, and John Wayne, who was at his most romantic opposite a strong leading lady, like Marlene Dietrich in *The Spoilers*. It is impossible to discuss Robert Niro as a leading man without also discussing him as a leading actor. Humphrey Bogart was for years one of Warner Brothers' stable of gangsters before he became a romantic figure in his forties through roles such as Sam Spade in *The Maltese Falcon* and Rick in *Casablanca*. Although many of Albert Finney's roles – in *Saturday Night and Sunday Morning* and *Two for the Road*, for instance – are romantic ones, he prefers to be regarded as a straight actor and his real love is the stage. Conversely, Laurence Olivier is so widely known as a consummate stage actor that it is often forgotten that his dashing good looks made him a fully fledged romantic idol before the war, in films like *Wuthering Heights* and *Rebecca*.

Often, too, leading men will take on parts that attack the popular conception of their image. I still tend to think of Robert Redford as the Kennedyesque character in *The Candidate*. Sexy, successful and photogenically pretty, in that film he inverted all those desirable characteristics to show the less worthy ones underneath, just as Hitchcock had done for Cary Grant's image in *Notorious* and *North by Northwest* and for James Stewart in *Rear Window* and *Vertigo*, and as Max Ophüls did for Louis Jourdan in *Letter from an Unknown Woman*.

Looking back with this in mind, there is no doubt that certain directors and leading men have a perfect chemistry, a symbiotic relationship, like that of Martin Scorsese and Robert De Niro. Likewise, the great point about Gary Cooper, who was used by an enormous number of great directors, was that he could be used by each of them in a particular way. Cooper was not a man with one face, but many different faces, as perceived by different directors.

Just as the image of a particular actor can be successfully turned on its head by a director, so, too, can the concept of the leading man with all the expectations of an audience that depend on it: William Holden's gigolo/heel in *Sunset Boulevard*, and the roles of Richard Gere in *American Gigolo* and Jon Voight in *Midnight Cowboy*

are all perfect examples. Howard Hawks remade Ben Hecht's stage comedy *The Front Page*, with Rosalind Russell cast in the 'leading man' role, opposite Cary Grant, in *His Girl Friday*. Gene Kelly as Don in *Singin' in the Rain* satirized the leading men of the old silents, who know the importance of image: 'Dignity, always dignity!' More recently, homage was paid to Bogart by Jean-Paul Belmondo in *Breathless*, and Woody Allen in *Play It Again, Sam*, while in *My Favourite Year* the Peter O'Toole character is a roistering, swashbuckling, drunken tribute to Errol Flynn – or, as some would have it, to John Barrymore.

There is also a delicious element of chance in the creation of screen heroes. The fact that the great stars could not possibly appear in all the films intended for them gave less prototype replacements wonderful opportunities to flex their romantic muscles. Joel McCrea was always dogged by the line, 'He got all the parts that Gary Cooper turned down'. Paul Newman started his career as a Brando clone. Gable got his role in *It Happened One Night* only after Robert Montgomery and Fredric March both passed on it, Michael Sarrazin turned down the part taken by Jon Voight in *Midnight Cowboy* and Jack Nicholson shot to stardom when Rip Torn pulled out of *Easy Rider*.

Among contemporary leading men, I think only the roles of Woody Allen could not go to several other actors. Robert Redford might have remained just another handsome California blond if Marlon Brando, Steve McQueen and Warren Beatty had not all refused the role of the Sundance Kid. John Travolta passed up on *American Gigolo*, and the part went to Richard Gere. The same holds true of certain performances of almost mythical status. George Raft thought it was bad luck to die on the screen and only then did his part in *High Sierra* go to Humphrey Bogart; Raft was also approached for Sam Spade in *The Maltese Falcon*, but declined because he lacked confidence in the young director, John Huston.

I can chart my adolescence by the leading men in my life; I think most people can. Whenever I told friends and colleagues I was writing a book about leading men their immediate reaction was to rattle off the names of their own favourites; perhaps the most interesting thing is that we rarely chose the greats. At twelve, I was in love with a minor British star called Michael Rennie – he looked a bit like Montgomery Clift and a bit like

Charlton Heston — and I cried for days after I saw him in *The Lost World* because it was in colour and I had never realized his hair was grey. I was also in love with Tab Hunter because I had seen his picture in 'Photoplay', just as Judy Garland, gazing at Clark Gable's photo and singing 'Dear Mr Gable, you made me love you . . .', had fallen for him.

In those days, the early sixties, our town still boasted a cinema, the Century, and after I had got over Michael Rennie's hair, it became the temple in which I worshipped Charlton Heston, sobbing into a handkerchief when *El Cid* made his final ride along the shoreline. I thought he was the epitome of all that was noble and romantic but above all *good*, the only figure of comparable virtue being Gregory Peck.

Then I became a discerning teenager. My boyfriend and I went to see *Tom Jones*, but all my concentration was on Albert Finney rolling around in the hay. That was followed by *The Great Escape*, Steve McQueen, the bike and the barbed wire. I loved him precisely because he wasn't good or noble, like Charlton Heston, but mad and rebellious. Finally came *The Graduate*, with little, beaky-nosed Dustin Hoffman breaking into the church to grab Katharine Ross in the nick of time before she married the wrong man. It was the most romantic gesture I had ever seen and some years later, as I stood at the altar, even though I very much wanted to marry the man I was standing next to, I saw myself fleetingly as Katharine Ross waiting for Hoffman to crash in and drag me away on a bus.

The recollection of personal favourites is also a highly pleasurable exercise in nostalgia. Many wonderful moments have resurfaced in my memory thanks to this book. I remembered Eastwood's Man With No Name riding his mule on screen at the beginning of *A Fistful of Dollars*, Redford and Newman joining hands and jumping off the cliff in *Butch Cassidy and the Sundance Kid*, and Jimmy Stewart putting the steak back on the plate to close the confrontation between Lee Marvin and John Wayne in *The Man Who Shot Liberty Valance*. The moments with Jack Nicholson could fill these pages on their own.

Many of the prototypes first appeared in the thirties: Clark Gable was the earthy, ordinary guy, swaggering with sexual self confidence as he bore Vivien Leigh up the stairs in *Gone with the Wind*; Gary Cooper became the strong, silent hero who said 'Yup' and who embodied the values of the American West in *Mr Deeds Goes to Town*; James Stewart, amiable and gauche, was the over-optimistic boy-next-door, who cried 'I want to live' when angel Clarence Oddbody showed him how rotten the world would have been if he'd never been born in *It's a Wonderful Life*. There was also the earnest patriot, Henry Fonda, who tamed the West in *My Darling Clementine*, and the smooth, successful American male, Cary Grant. There were wicked but lovable gangsters like James Cagney, and more menacing ones, like George Raft, whose real-life criminal connections added to his scary charm. European actors became associated with good breeding, graceful manners and sexy charm through Charles Boyer, Ronald Colman and Leslie Howard, whose places would later be taken by other elegant continentals and suave, witty Englishmen, such as David Niven, Rex Harrison, Michael Wilding, Louis Jourdan and Jeremy Irons.

Then, in the forties, came the wisecracking private eye and tough guy who operates within a strict moral code that is fair and just, but not necessarily legal. It was Humphrey Bogart in *The Maltese Falcon*, muttering 'When a man's partner's killed, he's supposed to do something about it'. A few years later, at the end of the forties, it was Robert Mitchum in *Out of the Past*, with a creased trenchcoat and a cigarette burning in his mouth. 'Is there a way to win?' asks *femme fatale* Jane Greer as she bets recklessly on the roulette wheel, and Mitchum's answer, about life in general, is 'There's a way to lose more slowly'. Neither Mitchum nor Bogart — nor for that matter John Garfield, another leading man of the forties who specialized in ex-cons and similar anti-heroes — were conventionally handsome. Their unpredicted audience appeal gave Hollywood the confidence to introduce a greater variety of leading men in the future, ugly yet beautiful like Dustin Hoffman and Al Pacino. Alan Ladd, the angelic killer, as ice cold as his opposite number Veronica Lake in *This Gun for Hire*, was another type altogether, and paved the way for Clint Eastwood's calmly violent avenging angel in Sergio Leone's trilogy of pasta Westerns, *A Fistful of Dollars, For a Few Dollars More* and *The Good, the Bad and the Ugly*, and Alain Delon's ruthless gangster in *Borsalino* and *The Sicilian Clan*.

With the emergence of Marlon Brando, James Dean and Montgomery Clift, all of whom had studied Method acting at Lee Strasberg's Actors' Studio in New York, came a very different and more honest depiction of masculinity. Their heroes, like those of the playwright Tennessee Williams, were flawed, complex, disturbed men whose dilemmas reflected the realities of life rather than Hollywood make-believe. James Dean, of course, had no time to be anything but a romantic hero, but even so, as Jim Stark, his character in *Rebel without a Cause*, he conveyed frightened isolation and a desperate need for love and understanding with which many teenagers could identify. It was the first time in the cinema that youth had found a hero of its own.

But Dean, like Brando and Clift, and, later, Newman and McQueen, was important in another way. Previously, most of the outstanding leading men had been screen naturals, with a fixed style of acting that came close to playing themselves. The technical innovation and mannerism of actors like Brando was of crucial relevance to the emergence of later 'acting' leading men like Jack Nicholson and Robert De Niro. In modern times, we have begun to see further changes in the presentation of leading men brought about by feminism — women being treated as subjects rather than objects. There were always strong leading ladies in the movies, for whom a leading man like Melvyn Douglas or Franchot Tone would be a debonair accessory, but this is not quite the same thing as the existence of a modern leading man who can be an aggressor and still not get the girl. If he does, it is his relevance to the girl which is important, rather than her place in life. Kris Kristofferson playing opposite Ellen Burstyn in *Alice Doesn't Live Here Anymore* is a good example; so, too, are Alan Bates in *An Unmarried Woman*, as everything Jill Clayburgh should want but she's still undecided about him, and Julie Christie's trio of lovers in *Far from the Madding Crowd*. Some of Dustin Hoffman's roles put the leading man in female circumstances. Ben is the passive object of Mrs Robinson's passions in *The Graduate*, in *Kramer vs Kramer* he battles against Meryl Streep to bring up their son, and in *Tootsie*, he literally becomes a leading lady. But it should be noted that in all of these roles Hoffman circumspectly steps back into straight male shoes in the end.

Nevertheless Hoffman's roles are in direct counterpoint to those which concern what Sam Shepeard describes as 'the macho psyche of the American male', the persona developed most clearly by Clint Eastwood in *Dirty Harry* and its sequels. Woody Allen is another interesting case because although he is going bald, wears specs and plays neurotics, and by all the old Hollywood criteria he should not be a leading man at all, he gets lots of glamorous women, both on and off screen, as in his classic partnership with Diane Keaton.

Perhaps real-life love enhances screen pairings, at least in the minds of the audience. There are two ways of looking at this. One is that when lovers play lovers they give off a glow that makes the whole movie memorable: Clara Bow and Gary Cooper in *Children of Divorce*, Marlene Dietrich and her various men — Gary Cooper in *Morocco*, James Stewart in *Destry Rides Again*, and John Wayne in *The Spoilers*. In the same way Clark Gable sparked with Loretta Young in *The Call of the Wild* and Joan Crawford in *Love on the Run* ('He had,' she later said, 'balls!'). The tradition continued after the war: Montgomery Clift and Liz Taylor were rumoured to be having an affair during the filming of *A Place in the Sun*, Steve McQueen and Ali MacGraw were together when they made *The Getaway*, as were Donald Sutherland and Jane Fonda in *Klute*. Most memorable of all though, are Bogart and Bacall.

On the other hand, maybe lovers playing lovers are often such a closed world that there's no room for someone in the audience to sneak in. And there is no doubt that emotionally charged pairings can be created without the personal electricity, as between Humphrey Bogart and Ingrid Bergman in *Casablanca*. Offscreen she apparently fancied him, but he wasn't interested. There is one constant, the romantic moment. It can defy definition, but it explains itself. I would not get very far if I tried to explain that Humphrey Bogart's attraction is in his lovely eyes and craggy face, but there is no need to if I simply remind you of the moment in *Casablanca* when he looks at Ingrid Bergman and says 'We'll always have Paris'.

THE SILENT ERA

The twenties was an era of larger-than-life figures – aviators, athletes, statesmen, jazz musicians and criminals – whose exploits and deeds dominated the rapidly developing media of the time. But movie idols, with their stylized beauty, remoteness and often inventively rewritten backgrounds, were the most fantastic of them all. Their very silence created an extraordinary aura of mystery and romance, and the extravagance of their gestures seemed to convey depths of passion and feeling beyond the experience of ordinary mortals.

The star system had developed in the previous decade. Since 1908, when movies had been the preserve of the dictatorial and monopolistic Motion Picture Patents Company, a combination of the ten leading film companies, there had been no stars. The Company believed, quite correctly, that a star would demand more money than an anonymous actor, and even the most popular performers were known either by the name of their character, like Little Mary, or that of their studio, like the Biograph Girl. But as the cinema shed its seedy image to become mass entertainment for America's aspiring materialist society, increasingly powerful and wealthy independent producers like Louis B. Mayer and William Fox, who were eager for a piece of the action, rightly figured that the extra cost of a star would be exceeded by box office returns.

The Biograph Girl, promoted under her real name, Florence Lawrence, by an immigrant clothes salesman, Carl Laemmle, became the first star and, within just a few years, Mary Pickford and Charlie Chaplin were commanding million-dollar contracts. Movie actors became glamorous personalities whose lives and loves were national gossip, publicity departments sprang up

in response to the public's rapturous curiosity, and 'Photoplay', the first fan magazine, which was founded in 1912, spawned scores of imitators.

By the beginning of the twenties, Hollywood was reflecting the manners and standards of post-war emancipated women, who had experienced independence through war-work, finally won the right to vote and were unwilling to return to an existence that revolved merely around domestic issues: they now expected jobs, smoked and drank, wore make-up – but no corsets – and hitched up their skirts. Scott Fitzgerald wrote of a younger generation that had 'All gods dead, all wars fought, all faith in man shaken'. The new freedom was also expressed in relaxed sexual attitudes. As the publicity handout for *The Sheik*, 1921, phrased it in a way which would have been completely unacceptable before the war, 'He wanted only one thing, and she knew what it was, and it would only be a matter of time before he got it.' So Valentino, who became for his contemporaries 'the symbol of everything wild and wonderful and illicit in nature', embarked on his brief but phenomenal career. Men copied his sleek black cap of hair, his swooning poses and his steamy love-making: back seats of cars transformed themselves into perfumed tents, newspaper editorials thundered about the influence of foreign Lotharios on wholesome young Americans and there was a spate of Valentino clones, like Ricardo Cortez, Rod La Rocque and Antonio Moreno.

Valentino was not the only influence on male style. Douglas Fairbanks Sr, all American pep and go, combined the athleticism of an Olympic champion with the moral code of a boy scout. He was the ideal healthy man, fighting off the sapping effects of the continentals. There was also boyish, Ramon Novarro, whose ardour was gentler and less threatening than that of Valentino, and John Gilbert, whose devil-may-care virility foreshadowed the qualities of men like Clark Gable, Errol Flynn and Gérard Philipe. Although Gilbert began as a Latin lover, his successful transfer to become Garbo's ardent partner may have restored to American men the self-confidence they lost during the phase when the exotic lover was all.

Meanwhile, films became spicier. The new plush movie palaces brought in an audience who were prepared to enjoy films that dwelt on the material, rather than the spiritual, joys of existence. Richard Barthelmess might have personified the Victorian tradition of innocence and purity in films like *Tol'able David*, 1921, but other pictures actually dared to admit that lust was a forgivable, maybe even pleasurable, impulse, and that married people who had eyes for others were not necessarily either immoral or miserable. Clergy and laymen might launch censorship drives to curb the morally reprehensible excesses of the new entertainment, but it did nothing to prevent the customers from coming in.

The ambiguities on screen were soon followed by juicy off-screen scandal. In the early twenties, Hollywood was shattered by a series of events which demonstrated its vulnerability to attack by moralists. Fatty Arbuckle was tried for the involuntary manslaughter of Virginia Rappe, who was found mauled in a room after his party in a San Francisco hotel. Although he was found not guilty, he was made a scapegoat and banned from pictures by nervous producers. In the same way, Wallace Reid's sudden death in 1923 was followed by scandal when it was discovered that he had been taking drugs that were readily available around the film world. As the film capital became synonymous with mass misbehaviour on a grand and titillating scale, the industry hastily decided to censor itself, rather than hand over to the zealous outside agencies who were queuing for the job, and offered a salary of $100,000 a year to Postmaster-General, Will Hays, to run Motion Picture Producers and Distributors of America Inc., an organization which would regulate the ethics of the film industry. Known as the Hays Office for short, it enveloped Hollywood with an atmosphere of anodyne propriety, which has nevertheless produced films of far greater subtlety.

RUDOLPH VALENTINO

Sixty years after his death, Valentino's name is still synonymous with steamy foreign passion, and he remains the erotic phenomenon with whom his successors are inevitably compared. But because his acting style, spawned by the demands of silent films, now looks almost farcical we tend to forget the staggering impact he had on his contemporaries. His magnetism lay in his ability to combine high-voltage eroticism with an underlying *politesse*; he might seduce well brought up young ladies in thrillingly unthinkable ways, but the two of them would then live happily ever after. Valentino's quintessential role was as Sheik Ahmed Ben Hassan to Agnes Ayres's Lady Diana in *The Sheik*, a high-romance drama which provided post-war audiences with the perfect paradigm of romantic-sexual escapism. His raw wooing of Lady Diana, half-draped and liquid-eyed, with nostrils open at full throttle, was a star turn which exemplified Valentino's sexual attraction as both predator and haven.

The son of a southern Italian vet, Rudolph Valentino had arrived alone in the USA at the age of eighteen, and then had to serve a long Hollywood apprenticeship playing romantic baddies in a series of unmemorable films before he was launched in 1921 by *The Four Horsemen of the Apocalypse*, one of Metro's biggest ever successes, in which director Rex Ingram cast him as Julio, a debonair wastrel who redeems himself in the First World War. *The Sheik* brought Valentino a passionate female following that has never been equalled, and, for five years, he was the screen's great lover in huge box-office successes like *Blood and Sand*, *The Eagle* and *The Son of the Sheik*, although other pictures such as *Monsieur Beaucaire* and *A Sainted Devil* were more tepidly received, probably because he was playing more effeminate characters.

Equally important for both the studio and his audiences, Valentino's per-

LEFT: publicity portrait for *A Sainted Devil*, 1924

14

sonal life did not live up to his screen image. His first marriage, to Jean Acker, lasted only one day, while his second wife, Natasha Rambova, hen-pecked him unmercifully; towards the end of his life, he became an object of heterosexual male contempt, con-demned in the press as a Pink Powder Puff. There has been much sub-sequent speculation about Valentino's sexuality; whether Rambova, for in-stance, had lesbian traits that brought out the latent homosexuality in her husband, or whether Valentino was a forerunner of the contemporary androgynous male represented by David Bowie and Boy George. As it was, heavily in debt, and with his

LEFT: dancing with Natasha Rambova c. 1924
BELOW: *The Sheik*, 1921, with Agnes Ayres

career past its peak, Valentino succumbed to peritonitis in New York on 23 August 1926, at the age of thirty-one. His tragically early death was thus probably opportune. Thousands of grief-stricken women supplied a legendary funeral extravaganza, and his mythical status was ensured.

RIGHT: *A Sainted Devil*, 1924, with Nita Naldi
BELOW: *Monsieur Beaucaire*, 1924, with André Daven
OPPOSITE: *The Son of the Sheik*, 1926, with Vilma Banky

WALLACE REID

Wallace Reid was an early all-American boy – tall, blue-eyed and slightly rumpled – who spent much of his time on screen in daring car chases, his angular limbs dangling around racy old bangers like an extension of the machinery. Reid's style at the wheel earned him the nickname Good-time Wally, an unfortunate soubriquet, given his later private agonies: in 1919, at the peak of his career, he crashed on the way to a location and, as a result of morphine shots he used to numb the pain so he could continue shooting, he became an addict. The morphine quickly took its toll and Reid inflicted further damage by heavy drinking.

A movie career was very much in the family tradition; Reid made his debut aged four, in his parents' stage act, and his first movies were all made for the Chicago company for which his father worked as a screenwriter. He starred in, and sometimes directed, numerous productions for other companies, and wedded one of his regular leading ladies, Dorothy Davenport.

Reid's breakthrough was to come in 1915 in *The Birth of a Nation*, and over the next few years he became known as the King of Paramount, topping the bill in movies like *Valley of the Giants*, 1919, *The Affairs of Anatol*, and *Forever*, both 1921. The public liked him best, however, in a string of run-of-the-mill comedy thrillers built around his screen image as the dashing, amusing boyfriend that plain girls fantasize about bringing home to Mom. The reality, of course, was very different, and he died, aged only thirty-two, in a sanatorium. Reid's youthful death focused scandalized attention on Hollywood. Eventually its hell-raising image would lead to the introduction of the Hays Code.

LEFT: *The Affairs of Anatol*, 1921

OPPOSITE: *The Thief of Bagdad*, 1924, with Julanne Johnston

Fairbanks Sr was a perfect piece of human engineering, combining balletic vitality and excellent coordination with heart-stopping good looks: tumbling dark curls, a piratical grin and lots of sexy crinkles around the eyes. He was a considerable athlete and daring gymnast who never proposed to a girl in the ordinary way: his declarations of love or proposals of marriage were always preceded by a string of sword fights, perilous journeys and miraculous feats of mountaineering and horsemanship. He was also always terribly honourable about it, as in *The Thief of Bagdad* when he steals into the princess' bedroom with the confidence of a cat-burglar and the respectability of a vicar.

Fairbanks Sr's screen persona was that of the dashing, unpretentious, lovable young blade who had no hang-ups about anything — the complete antithesis of Valentino although, like him, he was in the fancy-dress trade, buccaneering his way through films like *Robin Hood, The Gaucho* and *The Iron Mask* in a magnificent selection of breeches, harem pants, thigh boots, buckles, belts and wide-brimmed hats. His swashbuckling epics fuelled the American need for romance and adventure and the appeal of his fantasy escapism was vast, not only to women, who longed to be rescued by him, but also to boys and men, who admired his aura of frolicsome good health and clean-living mischievousness. Valentino would have taken advantage of a girl; Doug's whole persona was wrapped about the fact he would not. Even fathers would have been content to let their daughters leave the house with him at night. His success and popularity on screen was made more heady by his romance with Mary Pickford, America's Little Sweetheart, and despite the fact that they both had to ditch their respective spouses in order to marry in 1920, their popularity was heightened rather than

ABOVE: *The Three Musketeers*, 1921, with Barbara La Marr
RIGHT: *The Black Pirate*, 1926

tarnished by the union. Thousands of adoring fans made their European honeymoon resemble a royal procession, and they went on to become the First Family of Hollywood.

Fairbanks himself had had a fairly unconventional family life. The youngest of three sons, who were all devoted to their mother, a Southern beauty who had been married three times, he lacked a father figure on whom to model himself, which perhaps explains why he retained the persona of a boy well into adult life. The family was a very close one and both John and Robert, his two elder brothers, later worked in Doug's film empire.

Young Fairbanks capitalized on his childhood passion for acting after unsuccessful spells at Harvard — where he seems to have spent most of his time in the gymnasium — and on Wall Street. In 1915, he went West to make acrobatic dramas for the Triangle Film Company, earning $2,000 a week, before he moved on to his heroic parts in swashbuckling epics in the early twenties: a swordsman in *The Mark of Zorro*, D'Artagnan in *The Three Musketeers*, the outlawed Earl of Huntingdon in *Robin Hood*, and the prince of thieves in *The Thief of Bagdad*.

By the time sound came Fairbanks was in his forties and, although there was nothing wrong with his speaking voice, he was too firmly rooted in his era to adapt to the change of techniques required. By 1934 his marriage with Mary Pickford was over and he retired; only five years later he died of a heart attack. His films have endured as achievements of athletic imagination that can stand alongside modern equivalents like the ice dancing of Torvill and Dean and, despite the fancy dress, they can be viewed without hilarity or incredulity.

ABOVE: *The Private Life of Don Juan*, 1934
LEFT: *Don Q Son of Zorro*, 1925, with Mary Astor

RIGHT: *Taming of the Shrew*, 1929, with
Mary Pickford
BELOW: *The Black Pirate*, 1926

RICHARD BARTHELMESS

One of the handful of silent stars for whom there was life after sound, Richard Barthelmess made the transition through his acting ability as much as his tough good looks. His classic silent role was *Tol'able David*, in which he played the lead, a nice, dewy-eyed guy with an unsuspected streak of hardness and courage who wins through against the odds. It was the earliest example of a type that came to dominate the generation epitomized by Gary Cooper.

A New York boy who started off as an extra, Barthelmess took his first romantic lead in 1919, as the Yellow Man in D. W. Griffith's *Broken Blossoms*. He played opposite Lillian Gish who shared Barthelmess's gentle, innocent, Victorian beauty and his subtle emotional restraint. The two were paired again one year later in *Way Down East* with its final dramatic sequence when Gish struggles in an icy river while Barthelmess searches for her in the snowstorm, and rescues her just before she is carried over the deadly falls. Hard-working as well as handsome, he made films all through the twenties, and in 1927 managed to pull off two nominations as Best Actor at the first Academy Awards. After the arrival of sound, he accepted and carried off some risky and socially threatening roles, among them a junkie war veteran in *Heroes for Sale* and a disillusioned ex-airman in *The Last Flight*. His best talkie was *Only Angels Have Wings*, in which he played the part of a pilot who turns out to be not as chicken-hearted as he seems opposite Rita Hayworth. Made in 1939, towards the end of his career, it was a fine note on which to end.

RIGHT: studio portrait, c. 1935.
    Photographer William Walling

RAMON NOVARRO

Ramon Novarro's extraordinary zest in dashing costume parts made its strongest mark in his bicep-flashing performance in *Ben-Hur*, 1926. The son of a wealthy Mexican dentist, he shared Valentino's sloe-eyed handsome looks and vinyl hairdo, but his Latin lover was lighthearted, even tongue-in-cheek, compared to Valentino's rampant intensity. His boyish, winsomely strong-jawed face looked just great beneath a helmet.

Novarro first displayed his sword-twirling skills playing Rupert of Hentzau, the monocled baddie in *The Prisoner of Zenda* in 1922, and he went on to swashbuckle with virtuosity as the lead in *Scaramouche*. But it was as a love object, playing a native boy wild about a missionary's daughter, Alice Terry, that he won international worship in *Where the Pavement Ends* in 1923. The following year he established himself as an exotic in a shameless rip-off of *The Sheik* called *The Arab*, but his finest performance, in the title role of *The Student Prince*, opposite Norma Shearer, was not until 1927, the year after he made *Ben-Hur*.

At the beginning of the thirties his career began to fade and drinking did the rest. Like many of the silent stars in the strange new world of the talkies, he drifted into obscurity, resurfacing in the late forties in minor character roles. Retrospectively and rather unfairly pigeonholed as a grade-B Valentino, he died in retirement in 1968 in circumstances as tragic as those of any of his contemporaries. Rich, aging and never married, he was brutally murdered in October 1968 by two boys who just wanted his money.

OPPOSITE: studio portrait, c. 1929.
Photographer George Hurrell
ABOVE: *The Pagan*, 1929, with Dorothy Janis
LEFT: *Mata Hari*, 1931, with Greta Garbo

JOHN GILBERT

Gilbert became Valentino's undisputed successor as the great lover of the silent screen playing leading man to Greta Garbo in *Flesh and the Devil*. It was the start of one of the most romantic on-and-off screen liaisons ever; infatuated, he charmed her and proposed frequently, but she repeatedly turned him down and later denied that they had ever had an affair at all. On the screen he was impetuous and ardent, with a youthful sincerity and dashing smile that distinguished him from the rather more menacing Valentino, and his one imperfection, an awfully big nose, seemed to make him all the more appealing. In many ways he was a forerunner of Gable and Errol Flynn, with his uncomplicated, earthy, masculine energy. Ironically, though, Gilbert is now remembered less for his classic roles in silent films than for the tragic and rapid disintegration of his career at the onset of sound.

The son of a comic author, he used family connections to escape his unglamorous job as a rubber goods salesman, finding work as a bit player while he was still in his late teens. He moved up gradually via various unmemorable movies to steady employment as a leading man with Fox, then embarked on the most highly successful phase of his career with MGM, appearing in a succession of smash hits: *He Who Gets Slapped*, *The Merry Widow*, *The Big Parade* and *La Bohème*.

In 1927, Gilbert made his first film with Garbo, *Flesh and the Devil*, followed by *Love*, 1927, and *A Woman of Affairs*, 1929. He was deluged with fan mail and became the constant subject of gossip columns. Already married and divorced, his revenge on Garbo after she rejected him was to get married again, to someone else.

OPPOSITE: studio portrait, c. 1928.
Photographer Ruth Harriet Louise
ABOVE: *Wife of the Centaur*, 1924, with Aileen Pringle
LEFT: *La Bohème*, 1926, with Lillian Gish

His last silent film, *Desert Nights*, went out in 1929, and after that it was all downhill. His debut in the talkies in the balcony scene from 'Romeo and Juliet' in *The Hollywood Revue* of 1929 was not a success, but the real thumbs-down was given to *His Glorious Night*, for which audience reaction was divided between embarrassed sniggers and outright hilarity. Gilbert's failure was not, contrary to popular misconception, the inevitable result of a high, silly voice; in fact he spoke in a perfectly acceptable light tenor. In reality, it was his inability to master a new and different acting technique, and his increasingly sour personal conflict with Louis B. Mayer, that destroyed his career. He saw out his contract, even made reasonable films, but by then his confidence was in pieces. He had always been a heavy drinker, and in 1936 he drank himself to death.

ABOVE: *Flesh and the Devil*, 1927, with Greta Garbo

The dark-eyed Asther tempted some of Hollywood's greatest ladies away from the straight and narrow, most notably Greta Garbo, Pola Negri, Joan Crawford and Barbara Stanwyck. A pretty Swedish boy who originally entered films under the guidance of Garbo's mentor, Mauritz Stiller, he played exotic male siren to her fatal beauty twice in the same year, 1929: as a luscious Javanese prince trying to lure her from her rich, aging hubby in *Wild Orchids*, and a painter who runs off with her to the South Seas in *The Single Standard*.

Born in Scandinavia around the turn of the century, Asther began on the Copenhagen stage and made films in Germany before setting off to Hollywood in 1927. One of his first key romantic films was *Our Dancing Daughters*, 1928, with pure-as-driven-snow Crawford as the leading lady, in which his morals are corrupted by the Charleston. In the last few years of the silents he was one of Hollywood's most popular leading men. But Asther's strong Swedish accent made him a casualty of sound, though he studied English for months in order to try and convince MGM that he still had a future. Despite the sensuality of his performance as a Chinese warlord with erotic delights in store for a surprised Barbara Stanwyck, in *The Bitter Tea of General Yen*, 1933, his career fizzled out and he drifted into low-budget movies and truck-driving before returning to Sweden in 1959.

RIGHT: studio portrait, 1929.
Photographer Ruth Harriet Louise

JOHN BARRYMORE

One of the great tragi-romantic heroes of the silents in his heyday, Barrymore had a playful and ebullient screen personality, but also a self-destruct mechanism which had started with heavy drinking in his teens and ultimately drove him to the alcoholics' clinic. His stunningly patrician good looks gave him his nickname, the Great Profile, and he lived out his role as a dedicated ladies' man off stage, getting through four wives and numerous scandalous liaisons.

Barrymore came from a strong theatrical background. His father, who came from an English upper crust background, had appalled his family by going on the stage, and his mother was the actress Georgiana Drew. Her death, when John was only ten, devastated him and by the time he was fifteen he was already becoming dependent on alcohol. Although he started out working as a cartoonist, he followed family tradition and went on the Broadway stage in 1903. Barrymore built up a reputation as one of the most admired stage actors of his day and maintained a flourishing theatrical career for years after he had successfully moved into films. He achieved international stardom in 1920 with *Dr Jekyll and Mr Hyde*, and in 1924 made *Beau Brummel* opposite Mary Astor, who was then aged only seventeen. They embarked on a passionate romance, but two years later he fell in love with nineteen-year-old Dolores Costello, his leading lady in *The Sea Beast*, 1926, the screen adaptation of Melville's novel, 'Moby Dick'. He dropped Mary Astor and, at the age of forty-five, made Costello his third wife.

Not unexpectedly, Barrymore adapted to the talkies with effortless success, making his debut in *The Show of Shows* in 1929. His stage work now proved invaluable experience and the early thirties were a good time for him; in *Grand Hotel*, 1932, he played opposite Garbo, who later commented that Barrymore had the 'divine mad-

LEFT: publicity portrait for *Grand Hotel*, 1932

ness' of all great artists. But his drinking was increasingly causing problems. He now needed cue cards to remember his lines and after completing *Romeo and Juliet* he packed himself off to a clinic to dry out. His last years were beset by financial troubles which no doubt prompted his return to the stage where he acted, and fell down, in some very bad plays before he died of pneumonia in 1942.

LEFT: *Tempest*, 1928, with Camilla Horn
BELOW: *Eternal Love*, 1929, with Camilla Horn

RIGHT: *Grand Hotel*, 1932, with Greta Garbo
BELOW: *Twentieth Century*, 1934, with
      Carole Lombard
OPPOSITE: publicity portrait for *Twentieth*
      Century, 1934

THE STUDIO YEARS

Five Hollywood production studios dominated American cinema in the thirties. Paramount, Warner Brothers, 20th Century Fox, MGM and RKO – The Big Five – not only distributed their films worldwide, but also owned the cinema circuits, thereby controlling the entire life cycle of the movie. There was an irony in all this. Spawned by Europeans – the studio moguls were either Jewish immigrants, or the sons of Jewish immigrants – the movies were nonetheless America's mirror image of itself. The predominantly working-class audience fervently espoused the notion of the American dream as seen in the cinemas; they embraced its perceptions and models, including that of masculinity. But, in fact, that model was usually the parvenu's fantasy of tough, good-buddy American manhood.

Meanwhile, in the world outside, there were ominous developments: the rise of Nazism in Germany and the strengthening grip of Stalin in the Soviet Union. At the start of the decade, America had twelve million men unemployed. While memories of the First World War – the Great War – were still fresh, a second conflict became an inevitability. Little of this, however, is directly revealed in the films of the time. 'Remember My Forgotten Man', from *Gold Diggers of 1933*, might have been one of the most memorable Depression songs, but Hollywood more often saw itself as the lord of the dance, encouraging a willing audience to lose itself in opulent musical fantasy, lavish historical epics, screwball comedies, gangster films and literary adaptations. The stars tended to be like the movies: beautiful, romantic, exciting confections. Stills photographers sold the dreams that movies contained, reflecting the illusion of love, glamour and luxury that kept people believing in, and trying through comparison for, a better

existence. At the same time, the star treatment, and the growth of film types, like aviator Charles Lindbergh, reflected this blurring between fact and fiction. Men's fashion proliferated along the same lines: a Rolex Oyster watch became *de rigueur* because it was worn by a famous aviator. Male jewellery such as tiepins and cufflinks became widely worn, though this idea of the fashionable male as consumer died out by the end of the decade with the outbreak of war and a return to 'masculine' style.

Like every other member of the studio workforce, including the directors and scriptwriters, the actors were on contract and thus subject to despotic studio control. Every last detail of their careers was supervised by the dream factory and anyone who stepped out of line was smartly brought to heel. MGM's Louis B. Mayer, who thought his charges should act like royalty, once told off a star for eating in the studio dining room with a minor employee. At Warner Brothers, they worked their actors non-stop; a star could make seven films in a year. Studio despotism did not deter the thousands of hopefuls who turned up in Hollywood and signed away their bodies in exchange for the chance to become movie deities. But only a few – perhaps one per cent – made it, the remainder spending the best years of their lives waiting on tables.

In part this was thanks to the Hays Code, which sometimes resulted in a depiction of marriage that had little or nothing to do with the pleasures of the flesh. Movie-makers were barred from portraying any kind of hanky-panky that was unwedded, extra-marital, 'unnatural' or horizontal. There would be twin beds in the boudoir, and a gentleman always had to keep one foot on the floor. As it happened, the suggestion was just as erotic, if not more so, than the reality, in the hands of the right director.

The nickelodeon crowd and the silents had given way to sound and a more demanding audience. Valentino was dead, many silent stars had failed to adapt to the acting technique of sound, others still were simply obsolescent. In their place came an explosion of male types; a new generation at ease with the technology and prototypes they projected. Some were fashionable only during their decade, but a few transcended that to become mythical heroes whose style never dated and who are still imitated half a century or so later. In 1931, Clark Gable slapped rich bitch Norma Shearer around in *A Free Soul* and became the quintessence of 'rough trade' for women. Joan Blondell once said of him, 'he affected all females, unless they were dead'. When shy, sexy country boy Gary Cooper took on the city slickers in *Mr Deeds Goes to Town* in 1936, he established the image of the strong, silent, all-American hero. A handsome charmer who had been born Archie Leach in Bristol, England, became Cary Grant, distillation of the smooth, sophisticated American male. A telling point made by Donald Spoto in his excellent book 'Camerado' is that in Frank Capra's *It Happened One Night*, Gable showed men a new kind of role model, one

that depends on a man's attitude rather than his deeds; his tremendous sex-appeal and confidence gives him a totally unshakable awareness of his own abilities, and the Depression audiences found this encouraging. The same, perhaps, could be said for Grant, while Cooper gave optimism, through managing to remain a good man in a wicked world. But what also linked these three types was the response of their audience: they were not only adored by women in America and elsewhere around the world, but also had enormous influence over their fellow males. Together with their contemporaries, they heralded the New Man, of which there were several looks.

Masculinity now came in three basic types: it could either be sophisticated — Grant, Melvyn Douglas, William Powell or Robert Montgomery; earthy — Gable, Joel McCrea and John Wayne; or boyish or wholesome — Cooper, Henry Fonda, Jimmy Stewart. Sometimes, it was menacing, as with George Raft and James Cagney, and sometimes it was charmingly Gallic, Charles Boyer for instance, or tweedily British, Ronald Colman; more rarely it burst into song or dance, like Nelson Eddy, Fred Astaire and Bing Crosby. Occasionally it was celibate (Crosby as a priest). But it was very rarely effeminate, drunk or just plain nasty.

FREDRIC MARCH

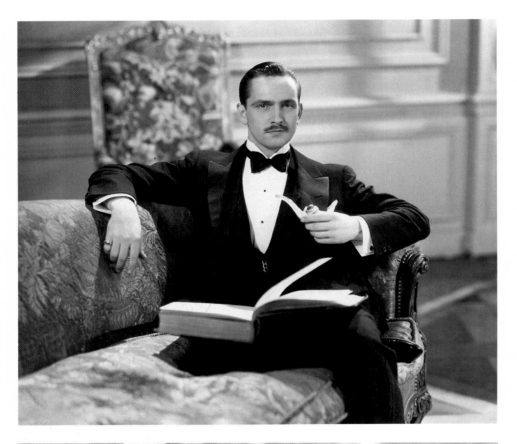

A subtle, expressive American, March was one of Hollywood's and Broadway's most distinguished performers, winning two Oscars – for *Dr Jekyll and Mr Hyde* in 1932, and *The Best Years of Our Lives*, 1946 – and making good films in a remarkable variety of genres over his forty-year career. During the thirties he played romantic lead opposite lots of glamorous ladies, notably Garbo in *Anna Karenina*, 1935, although he also worked on Broadway, often with his wife, Florence Eldridge. In much of his work he was essentially a reliable and durable support vehicle for his leading lady. His voice and looks were well suited to comedy, and he gave a notable performance in Ernst Lubitsch's *Design for Living*.

March had planned a career in banking, but decided while recovering from an attack of appendicitis in his early twenties that acting would be more fun. His film career took off after he recreated the role of John Barrymore, the Great Profile, in the screen version of *The Royal Family of Broadway* and he played the first of the fading film stars in *A Star Is Born*, 1937, leading the way for James Mason and Kris Kristofferson in later remakes. He demonstrated his versatility by taking on Carole Lombard in the screwball comedy *Nothing Sacred* in the same year. When he got too old to be a romantic hero he took on character roles with great distinction.

ABOVE: publicity portrait for
The Night Angel, 1931
LEFT: *Anna Karenina*, 1935, with Greta Garbo

OPPOSITE: *The Magic Flame*, 1927, with
Vilma Banky

Reserved and courteous, hands characteristically tucked in his pockets, Ronald Colman was British in the most charming way, projecting reliability without stuffiness and good manners without insincerity. Women found his wistful, faraway look — hinting at past tragedies bravely borne — and his dashing looks quite irresistible. In one of his most powerful performances as the nobly self-sacrificing Sidney Carton in *A Tale of Two Cities*, 1935, he forbore to declare his love for Elizabeth Allan, but typically did the 'far, far better thing' and died for her sake. It seemed entirely in character when, in the early thirties, he departed for 20th Century Fox after Sam Goldwyn opined that his acting would be all the better for a few drinks inside him.

Born in England and married to British actress Benita Hume, Colman never lost his European charm even though he settled and spent most of his working life in the USA. He established himself as a romantic hero of the silents and after getting his break opposite Lillian Gish in *The White Sister*, 1923, he and Vilma Banky became one of the great teams of the period in screen romances like *The Magic Flame*, 1927, and *Two Lovers*, 1928. His first major sound success was *Bulldog Drummond* in 1929 and his subsequent films were invariably suited to his aura of gentlemanly refinement, as in *Arrowsmith*, *The Masquerader*, *Bulldog Drummond Strikes Back* and *The Man Who Broke the Bank at Monte Carlo*.

Blessed with a gorgeous speaking voice, the witty and urbane Colman went on to become even more popular after the advent of sound. He adapted quickly to the restraint and understatement required, but he had to wait another twenty years for the industry's top prize, finally winning an Oscar towards the end of his career as the

ABOVE: studio portrait, c. 1929
RIGHT: *The Prisoner of Zenda*, 1937, with Madeleine Carroll
OPPOSITE: *Arrowsmith*, 1931, with Myrna Loy

Where Ronald Colman had a crisp middle-class accent, Clive Brook's appeal was handsome upper-class suaveness of the officer and gentleman variety; whether he was playing dukes, detectives or gangsters he always knew the right way to hold his knife and fork. He had served in the First World War, looked splendid in uniform and gave one of his finest performances as the officer and ex-lover of prostitute Shanghai Lily, Marlene Dietrich, in 1932 in *Shanghai Express*; his stylized mock heroism contrasting intriguingly with Dietrich's effortless aura of sexual threat.

Brook had learned his craft on stage before Hollywood discovered his potential as officer and gentleman material in a British film, *Woman to Woman*, 1923. His popularity took him to the USA where one of his most memorable roles was that of Rolls Royce, the upper-crust gangster and lover of Feathers, played by Evelyn Brent, in *Underworld*, 1927. He also portrayed Sherlock Holmes twice, and played the well-heeled stockbroker who married Tallulah Bankhead's low-living socialite in *Tarnished Lady*. When *Cavalcade*, Noël Coward's giant play about British class mores, was brought to the screen in 1933, he was the natural choice to play an 'ordinary' upper-class Englishman.

In the mid-thirties he returned to Britain and made several excellent films, such as *Convoy*, 1940, and in 1945 produced, directed and played the romantic lead in *On Approval*, a fizzing comedy which allowed him to shine as an Edwardian duke. He spent the rest of his working life appearing occasionally on television and the stage in Britain. He died in 1974.

RIGHT: *Shanghai Express*, 1932, with Marlene Dietrich

WILLIAM POWELL

William Powell's urbane and not-quite-decent image was enhanced by a pair of sensually droopy eyelids, underneath which his eyes would rove knowingly around the more interesting points of his leading ladies. In the thirties he won extraordinary popularity in *The Thin Man* series, playing one half of the much-loved husband-and-wife team, Nick and Nora Charles, Dashiell Hammett's sophisticated sleuths who were never short of a good line or the ice for their dry martinis. His persona shifted interestingly over his career, from his days of silent villains to Nora Charles's rather thrilling husband, and on to the irascible but kind-hearted father figure he played in *Life with Father*, towards the end of his career.

Powell played numerous baddies in the silent era, but his career only really took off with the arrival of sound, when he emerged as a skilled comedy actor who played well-mannered and fun-loving, but nevertheless slightly caddish, good guys — the type who would lead girls astray. He was amusing, glossy, sophisticated, sour, the personification of the best of thirties comedy. He and Loy teamed up with Spencer Tracy and Jean Harlow in *Libeled Lady*, 1936, a perfect vehicle for Powell's air of worldly *savoir-faire*, and he also played suave professional men turned sleuths again opposite Ginger Rogers in *Star of Midnight*, 1935, and Jean Arthur in *The Ex-Mrs Bradford*, 1936. His biggest acting success was as yet to come, however, playing the husband of Irene Dunne in *Life with Father*, for which he won an Academy Award nomination in 1947. As he grew old he moved on to character parts, and retired in 1955 after making his 95th film.

OPPOSITE: studio portrait, c. 1930
ABOVE: on set for *Reckless*, 1935, with
    Jean Harlow
LEFT: *Libeled Lady*, 1936, with Myrna Loy

HERBERT MARSHALL

Marshall had lost a leg in the First World War, though he disguised his disablement and his age – he was forty before his first serious venture into the cinema – successfully enough to develop into a romantic star as a member of Hollywood's European string. A gifted actor with traditional good looks, his speciality was that of the long-suffering and well-meaning husband whose wife treated him appallingly: he was pushed around by Greta Garbo in *The Painted Veil* in 1934, cuckolded by Melvyn Douglas and Marlene Dietrich in *Angel* in 1937 and 'killed' by arch-bitch Regina, Bette Davis, in *The Little Foxes*, 1941. Sympathetic women wanted to rescue him, perhaps secretly hoping that they, too, would get the chance to let their hair down and work out their anti-male feelings. However, he did not always play well-behaved saps; he was a fully-fledged romantic hero opposite Kay Francis and Miriam Hopkins in *Trouble in Paradise*, 1932, and had a light touch in comedy, even though he had an air of sobriety that clung to him from his early days of accountancy training.

As Marshall grew older his screen persona shifted to that of the attractive father figure, suave and experienced. As he had done with other leading men, Hitchcock inverted Marshall's persona to reveal its unattractive side, casting him as the smooth, paternal Nazi sympathizer in *Foreign Correspondent*, in 1940.

masculine qualities and strong aura of honesty were equally appealing to men.

Ironically, Cooper was British. His immigrant father, a judge who owned a ranch in Montana, earned enough to send young Frank — the 'Gary' came later — to England for a private school education, and Cooper kept a trace of the accent as a subtle clipping of his famous soft-spoken drawl. Cooper's private school period was indirectly beneficial in another way: his hip was damaged in a car accident and his long convalescence in Montana, during which he spent as much time as possible on horseback for his hip,

RIGHT: studio portrait, c. 1935.
Photographer Eugene Richee
BELOW: *Morocco*, 1930, with Marlene Dietrich

turned him into an excellent rider.

In fact, he began his film career as an extra in Westerns, falling off horses at $5 a time. By 1927 he was on contract to Paramount, where he won a minor role in *It*, and, just as significantly, the attention of Clara Bow. Although his off-screen romance with her did not last long, it launched him as a heart-throb and perfectly complemented his roles in a string of action pictures. Over the next few years, Cooper had several other well-publicized romances, including a turbulent relationship with Lupe Velez, his leading lady in *Wolf Song*, 1929. His reputation was that of the super virile stud of whom a friend

LEFT: portrait, c. 1936
BELOW: *Today We Live*, 1933, with Joan Crawford

once said, 'He was the greatest cocks-man who ever lived'. However, in 1933 he married a New York socialite, Veronica 'Rocky' Balfe, who turned a blind eye to her husband's subsequent entanglements with his leading ladies such as Marlene Dietrich and Ingrid Bergman. Their life-long union was threatened only once, by Cooper's love affair with an actress, Patricia Neal, when he was fifty and she was twenty-six.

By the end of the thirties, Cooper had risen to become the highest wage-earner in the United States and one of Hollywood's most powerful box-office draws. He reached the top, and stayed there, thanks to an output of consist-ently good films. Although he never troubled himself with more equivocal roles, he was both versatile and flex-ible within self-imposed limits, and he never parodied himself.

In *The Plainsman*, 1936, and *The Westerner*, 1940, his strength and simplicity perfectly suited the arche-typal Western hero, but he could also convey the melancholy detachment of a Hemingway hero in *A Farewell to Arms*, 1932. He turned in a skilled comic performance in *Mr Deeds Goes to Town*, 1936, the Frank Capra movie which put Cooper into American icon-ography for keeps as the man of humanism and virtue triumphing over the forces of violence and corruption. 'To get folks to like you,' he once said, 'I figured you had to sort of be their ideal. I don't mean a handsome knight riding a white horse, but a fellow who answered the description of a right guy.' He may have been unlucky when Goldwyn refused to loan him out for the part of Rhett Butler in *Gone with the Wind*, but his performance in *Sergeant York*, 1941, as a mumbling Tennessee boy who turns from paci-fism to war gallantry, won him his first Oscar. Cooper, in short, could per-

ABOVE: *Beau Geste*, 1939, with Ray Milland
RIGHT: *One Sunday Afternoon*, 1933, with
    Fay Wray
OPPOSITE: studio portrait, 1932.
    Photographer Clarence Sinclair Bull

sonify many facets of America's vision of itself and he was used by an incredible variety of directors – Capra, Hawks, von Sternberg, Wyler, Lubitsch, Vidor and Mann among them.

Though Cooper's first forays into romantic movies were less than successful – as Paramount's 'glorious young lovers', he and Fay Wray never really clicked – he overcame his initial woodenness to star with a wide range of leading ladies, from Marlene Dietrich in *Morocco*, 1930, to Joan Crawford in *Today We Live*, 1933, and ten years later he was nominated for an Oscar with Ingrid Bergman for their chemistry in *For Whom the Bell Tolls*, one of the greatest romantic movies to come out of Hollywood. They played together again in *Saratoga Trunk*, by which time Cooper had matured to an attractive cragginess.

The post-war years were less easy for Cooper. His films were variable in quality and his autumn-to-spring affair with Patricia Neal brought a four-year separation in his marriage. But in 1952 came *High Noon*, in which he stood as the embodiment of moral as well as physical courage. The control, determination and subtlety of his performance won him his second Academy Award. It was not his last Oscar; in April 1961, when he was dying of cancer, he was honoured by the film industry with a Special Academy Award for outstanding services. Less than a month later, he was dead.

OPPOSITE: publicity portrait for *For Whom the Bell Tolls*, 1943
ABOVE: *Saratoga Trunk*, 1945, with Ingrid Bergman
LEFT: *Mr Deeds Goes to Town*, 1936, with Jean Arthur

JOEL McCREA

McCrea was an amiable, athletic and dependable American hero who made up for what he lacked in wits with courage and endurance and he immediately appealed to the ordinary man who admired achievement but suspected cleverness. He shared Gary Cooper's bony good looks if not his air of intellectual perception — and now tends to be pigeonholed as the actor who got the parts Cooper turned down — but his uncomplicated and overt physicalness made him seem more easily attainable.

McCrea's cosy earnestness and integrity were particularly exploited by two outstanding directors, Alfred Hitchcock and Preston Sturges. He played his most interesting role in Hitchcock's *Foreign Correspondent*, 1940, starring as an exceptionally dull-witted but likable reporter who, lacking the street wisdom to anticipate danger, is forced to resort to his enormous reserves of courage for impromptu situations. For Preston Sturges he played a Hollywood director turned vagrant, innocently overwhelmed by real life, alongside Veronica Lake in *Sullivan's Travels*, 1941. He also played the lead in *Buffalo Bill*, 1944, for William Wellman, although it was only in the fifties that he began to star in numerous small-budget Westerns and build his reputation as the perennial cowboy hero. This was summed up in Sam Peckinpah's nostalgic tribute, *Ride the High Country*.

LEFT: publicity portrait for *Adventure in Manhattan*, 1936

OPPOSITE: studio portrait, 1936.
Photographer Ted Allan

and won numerous top military honours, including the Distinguished Service Medal. No demon lover in his private life, he remained a stolid bachelor until, in his early forties, he met his wife, Gloria, through Gary Cooper.

Some of Stewart's strongest postwar performances were given in Westerns. His image, like that of Cooper, communicated the sense of honesty and patriotism required of the Western hero: he was powerful hunting down his own brother in *Winchester 73* and moving as the husband of an Indian girl (Debra Paget) in *Broken Arrow*, both made in 1950, but engagingly naive in *The Man Who Shot Liberty Valance*, 1962. In a quite different vein, his humour saved *The Glenn Miller Story*, 1954, from drowning in its own sentimentality. One of his most appealingly funny performances was in *Harvey*, 1950, as Elwood P. Dowd, a friendly soak who has regressed to childhood by postulating a giant rabbit as his invisible playmate. Stewart's endearing charm was also used intriguingly by Hitchcock, who cast him well against type as the voyeur in *Rear Window*, 1954.

ABOVE: portrait, c. 1938
LEFT: *It's a Wonderful Life*, 1947, with Donna Reed

HENRY FONDA

One of Hollywood's most earnest heroes, Fonda had a chiselled sobriety perfectly suited to the noble idealism of his roles as representative of the national spirit and conscience. His great Americans, whether military, Western or political, struggled against anarchy and disorder. He played a youthfully solemn Abe Lincoln in John Ford's *Young Mr Lincoln*, 1939, the strong-minded symbol of frontier justice, Wyatt Earp in *My Darling Clementine*, and Tom Joad in *The Grapes of Wrath*, a key film of conscience. It was perhaps appropriate that in the sixties, when the USA had lost its innocence, the most important symbol of its goodness played a vicious sadist, in *Once Upon A Time In The West*, 1968.

Fonda's gift for conveying noble idealism and human unworthiness at the same time made him equally strong in more equivocal roles, playing men who had the courage to attempt heroic tasks without necessarily being up to them. He could be angry or confused without compromising his virility: his voice, with its homely Nebraska twang, cracked with honest, manly emotion when he was overwhelmed with feeling. Fonda very rarely got caught in a clinch and when he kissed, it was usually the official married peck. Marriage for him was usually a duty or a cerebral affair, though the closing wedding scene in *My Darling Clementine* was one of the most moving images ever of marriage and stability taming the Wild West.

Fonda appeared frequently on the Broadway stage and, at the age of seventy-three, was an enormous success in a one-man show as the famous liberal lawyer, Clarence Darrow. He died only a year after winning an Oscar for his performance in *On Golden Pond*, as the irascible but still bravely unbowed father.

OPPOSITE: studio portrait, c. 1936
ABOVE: publicity portrait for *My Darling Clementine*, 1946
LEFT: *That Certain Woman*, 1937, with Bette Davis

GEORGE RAFT

JOHN WAYNE

Sleek, solemn and full of sexual menace, Raft's most successful screen persona was that of the vicious gangster. Born in a rough area of New York, he was said to have gambling, casino and underworld connections, which added to his thuggish charm.

His image as a gangster was crystallized in 1932 in *Scarface*, as the coin-tossing baddie Rinaldo, bumped off by a vicious killer, Tony Camonte (Paul Muni). However, he did get a chance to play good baddies in *Each Dawn I Die* and *Invisible Stripes*, both in 1939. In *Manpower*, 1941, he was the object of Marlene Dietrich's straying passions. Billy Wilder got Raft to satirize himself as Spats, the Chicago gangster, in *Some Like It Hot*, 1959.

BELOW: studio portrait, c. 1939

Wayne starred in some of the greatest Westerns ever made, notably the John Ford trilogy, *Fort Apache*, *She Wore A Yellow Ribbon* and *Rio Grande*, and became the USA's most historically important star. He is usually remembered as hard-fighting and sexy in a rugged, authoritarian way, offering tough gallantry to all women on principle. However, in his best-known starring role, in *Stagecoach*, he was in the sensitive pin-up mould, and in *The Searchers*, later on in his career, he was ruthlessly unforgiving and ready to kill. A big but graceful, ugly-beautiful man, he found a good match in strong leading ladies like Marlene Dietrich, in *Seven Sinners*, 1940.

ABOVE: publicity portrait for *Conflict*, 1936
OPPOSITE: studio portrait, c. 1936

From the moment Cagney shoved half a grapefruit into Mae Clarke's face in *The Public Enemy*, 1931, his ebullient delinquency was irresistible. He was the quintessential gangster of the cinema; a cruel hoodlum with a disturbing childlike look and an inimitable staccato style of speech fired off like the emptying of a machine gun who went around wrecking speakeasies, breaking out of jail, roughing up women and generally behaving very badly indeed.

But under the tough exterior was an underlying vulnerability which surfaced in the desire to be mothered or to set a good example, as in his gangster role in *Angels With Dirty Faces*, 1938. His appeal lay in the idea that under the gangster there lurked a vulnerable kid: in *White Heat*, 1949, he delivered a telling farewell to the world, crying 'Top of the world, Ma!', discharging his gun into a gas tank and blowing himself to eternity.

Cagney's childhood background was as formatively rough as that of any of his characters. Born in Manhattan's Lower East Side in 1899, he established an early reputation for tough street fighting and at one time aspired to a boxing career, but in fact entered show business as a vaudeville dancer in drag. His fifth film, *The Public Enemy*, made him a star and he carried through the gangster persona in films like *Lady Killer*, 1933, and *The Roaring Twenties*, 1939, to become one of the top ten box-office draws. Underlying the persona was a neurotic sexuality, nervy and jumpy, which became positively psychotic in *White Heat*, bridging the gap between thirties tough guy and fifties neurotic hero.

Having retired in 1961, he emerged over twenty years later to play the police chief in *Ragtime*.

ABOVE: *The Public Enemy*, 1931, with Jean Harlow
RIGHT: *Picture Snatcher*, 1933, with Alice White

OPPOSITE: studio portrait, 1937. Photographer Laszlo Willinger

In *Broadway Melody of 1938*, Judy Garland gazes at a photograph and sings 'Dear Mr Gable, you made me love you', a sentence which mirrored the sentiments of thousands of fans of the time. Gable's stupendous charisma made him King of Hollywood, carried him through the thirty years of changing fashion in masculinity, and brought him a series of classic leading roles, stretching from *Red Dust* in 1932 to *The Misfits*, his last film in 1961. Gable was essentially a man of the people: a plain-spoken, tough boy from small-town America who never put on unnatural airs or graces, and had little time for women who did; look at the way he slapped rich bitch Norma Shearer around in *A Free Soul*.

Gable was particularly proud of one of his acting techniques – while his female co-stars melted under his lusty, lingering gazes, he was actually thinking of a piece of prime, juicy steak. The technique certainly worked. Cynical, self-assured and extremely sexy, his host of leading ladies reads like a roll-call of all-time greats: Mary Astor, Jean Harlow, Greta Garbo, Joan Crawford, Vivien Leigh, Carole Lombard, Hedy Lamarr and Marilyn Monroe. While he could be passionate and protective, he never swooned over his women, instead cheerfully treating them as equals and expecting them to reciprocate with honesty and integrity – or face the consequences. In one of his first big successes, *It Happened One Night*, 1934, his thumb-on-the-nose reporter typically fell in with a society miss (Claudette Colbert), refused to treat her like a lady and won her over, almost literally at the final curtain, when the blanket that primly divided their room came tumbling down. His direct earthiness and offer of a certain kind of sexual democracy was universally appealing. He also had a huge

ABOVE: *Dancing Lady*, 1933, with Joan Crawford
LEFT: *No Man of Her Own*, 1932, with
    Carole Lombard
OPPOSITE: studio portrait, c. 1931.
    Photographer George Hurrell

years his senior who gave him coaching and helped him up the movie ladder, and then to Ria Langham, another older woman, he diverted himself over the next decade with numerous fleeting affairs and one-night stands with a maelstrom of females both celebrated and obscure. One of his entanglements was with Joan Crawford, who later remarked, 'He had balls', but the tough, beautiful hoyden Carole Lombard, whom he married in 1939, was probably his one great love. They had no chance to become disenchanted: early in 1942,

LEFT: *After Office Hours*, 1935, with
    Constance Bennett
BELOW: *Strange Cargo*, 1940, with
    Joan Crawford

at the age of thirty-four she was killed in a plane crash. He went looking for her in the wreckage, utterly traumatized by her death.

By that time, Gable had reached the peak of his career. He had drifted through various jobs – salesman, lumberjack, reporter and truck driver – and survived rejection from both Warner Brothers and MGM (after John Barrymore had suggested they screen-test him) before becoming a major star in the early thirties. He turned in some crackling love scenes with Jean Harlow in *Red Dust*, 1932, won an Academy Award for his performance in the Frank Capra comedy, *It Happened One Night*, and gave a lovely performance opposite Jeanette MacDonald in *San Francisco*. His ultimate movie was still to come. Margaret Mitchell, the author of *Gone With The Wind*, is reputed to have had Gable's screen persona in mind when she created the character of 'Frankly, my dear, I don't give a damn' Rhett Butler; certainly, fiction and flesh are hard to distinguish and Gable's portrayal is a crucial factor in the success of Selznick's film. Unchivalrous, baldly lustful, knowing and cocking a snook at all social and emotional pretension, the Butler/Gable character overshadowed many modern screen heroes.

Shortly after Lombard's death – her last cable to him read, 'Pappy, you'd better join this man's army' – Gable finished his shooting commitments on *Somewhere I'll Find You* and enlisted as a private in the air force, remaining there for the rest of the war. He teamed up with Greer Garson, whom he loathed, for his return to the screen in *Adventure*, 1945, but it was a failure and after that he made few memorable films. His popularity remained as strong as ever, but, by now middle-aged, he was uneasy in the role of romantic male lead that producers persisted in assigning to him. His most

ABOVE: *Red Dust*, 1932, with Jean Harlow
RIGHT: *Red Dust*, with Mary Astor
OPPOSITE: *Saratoga*, 1937, with Jean Harlow

successful post-war film was, perhaps, *Mogambo*, 1953, John Ford's
remake of *Red Dust*, playing opposite
Ava Gardner and Grace Kelly. Meanwhile, his private life continued chop-
pily. He married twice more, first to
Sylvia, Lady Ashley and then to Kay
Spreckels, who looked like Carole
Lombard and produced Gable's only
child, a son, after his death.

Gable's last performance, tough,
earthily sexy and never more poignant,
as the aging cowboy lover of Marilyn
Monroe in *The Misfits*, 1961, was
hailed by the critics as the outstanding
performance of his career. Full of
ironies about aging, love and male
vitality, it can be seen as Gable review-
ing his own masculinity. He died in
November 1960, a few weeks after
shooting finished.

OPPOSITE: *Gone with the Wind*, 1939, with
     Vivien Leigh
ABOVE: *The Misfits*, 1961
LEFT: *Mogambo*, 1953, with Grace Kelly

DOUGLAS FAIRBANKS Jr

The studios didn't have to look far for a Douglas Fairbanks Sr clone; they had Doug Jr, the son from his first marriage to Anna Beth Sully. American by birth and British by culture, Doug Jr gravitated towards Hollywood in the silent era against his father's wishes, but made little headway until the advent of sound, when he succeeded to his father's buccaneering persona and swashbuckling role despite evidence that his glossy charm was more suited to drawing-room roles. He produced a notable performance as the caddish soldier of fortune, Rupert of Hentzau, in John Cromwell's version of *The Prisoner of Zenda*, 1937, and was one of three soldier pals (Cary Grant and Victor McLaglen were the others) holding the fort – and Joan Fontaine – in the British imperialist yarn, *Gunga Din*.

A well-known socialite, married first to Joan Crawford, Fairbanks Jr was also repeatedly cast in more debonair parts, playing the carefree admirer of Irene Dunne in *Joy of Living*, the student holiday-camp worker amongst man-crazy girls in *Having Wonderful Time*, opposite Ginger Rogers, and with Danielle Darrieux in *The Rage of Paris*, all in 1938. In the forties, he appeared in a series of acclaimed adventure yarns like *Sinbad The Sailor*, 1947, but somehow, perhaps because he was neither wholly British nor wholly American, Doug seemed permanently out of tune with the times. At the start of the fifties he retired from film-making to produce and sometimes play in the television series, 'Douglas Fairbanks Presents'.

LEFT: *Gunga Din*, 1939, with Joan Fontaine
OPPOSITE: publicity portrait for *The Prisoner of Zenda*, 1937

BING CROSBY

NELSON EDDY

Crosby became one of the USA's top box-office draws in the forties, as the crooning lead who starred in the classic musical *Birth of the Blues* and played the smarmy pipe-smoker restraining Bob Hope's passions in the 'Road' series with Dorothy Lamour. He was given a more challenging role as the genial, whisky-swigging Father O'Malley in *Going My Way,* for which he won an Academy Award in 1944.

In the more austere, post-war world, he was a reassuring hero who conveyed the message that life's problems could be solved with a smile, a song and a round of golf; and in the fifties he made a comeback with *White Christmas*, 1954, and *High Society*, 1956. He liked playing golf and was in mid-round when he died in 1977.

BELOW: *Birth of the Blues*, 1941, with Mary Martin

A romantic, winsomely handsome charmer, Nelson Eddy was only a minor film success till MGM teamed him with Jeanette MacDonald in *Naughty Marietta* in 1935, and they sang 'Ah, Sweet Mystery of Life' at each other across a crowded room. Although legend has it that neither of them liked the other very much, they became America's Sweethearts and the public crowded into *Rose Marie*, 1936, *Maytime*, 1937, and the seven other costume musicals they made together. Eddy's screen career nosedived after the partnership split up in the forties, but he kept on singing until he died after a stroke on stage during a tour of Australia.

ABOVE: publicity portrait for *Maytime*, 1937, with Jeanette MacDonald

FRED ASTAIRE

Genial and elegant but ultimately elusive as a screen persona, Astaire's bewitching power was in his movement. He was once described as the 'vertical expression of horizontal desire', and his legs were insured for $300,000. He headed for Hollywood after his elder sister, Adele, had retired from their dazzlingly successful dance partnership on Broadway and fortunately survived his first Hollywood screen test, which offered the discouraging verdict, 'Can't act. Slightly bald. Can dance a little'.

It was at RKO that he formed his legendary partnership with Ginger Rogers. No one has ever danced like them, before or since. Their extraordinary chemistry was explosive in movies like *The Gay Divorcee*, 1934, *Top Hat*, 1935, *Roberta*, 1935, and *Swing Time*, 1936. She could not match his skill but brought colour and sensuality to his airy grace, or as Katharine Hepburn put it, 'He gave her class, she gave him sex'.

When Ginger Rogers virtually gave up dancing in the late thirties, Astaire became debonair playboy consort to a series of leading ladies like Eleanor Powell, Rita Hayworth, Judy Garland, Cyd Charisse and Audrey Hepburn. There is a school of thought that after Rogers he was zero, but he had great sequences with Charisse in *The Band Wagon*, and was brilliant, as was Hepburn, in *Funny Face*. He remained as commanding and dominant as ever and when he was pitted against his great rival, Gene Kelly, in *Ziegfeld Follies*, 1946, he won on points.

Astaire went on to play convincing straight dramatic roles in later life such as *On The Beach*, 1959, and *The Towering Inferno*, 1974. In 1949 he received his special Academy Award for 'unique artistry and his contributions to the technique of motion pictures' — a long-winded way of saying he was magic.

RIGHT: publicity portrait for *Broadway Melody of 1940*

Howard brought to his roles as a beautifully spoken English gentleman a slightly dreamy, bashful air which suggested philosophical reflection and a charming shyness. He was perfectly cast and is always remembered as Ashley Wilkes, the young lover in *Gone With The Wind,* although he was in fact aged forty-five when he took the role.

Howard was first encouraged to dabble in local amateur dramatics by his mother Lillian while he was working in a bank — which he hated — after leaving public school. Later, when he was invalided out of the Cavalry with severe shell-shock during the First World War, he decided to try his luck as an actor, and by the late twenties, he was outstandingly successful on the stage on both sides of the Atlantic. His film career took rather longer to reach its peak: *Smilin' Through,* a 1932 weepie with Norma Shearer, established him as a heart-throb, but his first huge success was not until 1935 in Alexander Korda's *The Scarlet Pimpernel,* playing opposite Merle Oberon as the foppish but daring Sir Percy Blakeney. In *The Petrified Forest,* 1936, he recreated his stage role of the poetic stranger who befriends an idealistic young waitress, Bette Davis, before meeting his death at the hands of gangster Humphrey Bogart. It had in fact been Howard who insisted that the part be given to Bogart, rather than Edward G. Robinson, because of his stage performance, thus breaking Bogart in the gangster mould and establishing a life-long friendship.

Over the next few years Howard found more challenging parts: Romeo to Norma Shearer's Juliet; a New York accountant in the good 1937 Hollywood satire *Stand-In*; then a brilliantly successful Professor Higgins in the British *Pygmalion,* 1938, which he co-directed. He had reservations about taking on the role of Ashley Wilkes at

RIGHT: *The Scarlet Pimpernel,* 1935, with Merle Oberon

OPPOSITE: *Roberta,* 1935, with Ginger Rogers

the age of forty-five, but he was wonderful in the part, all refined integrity to Gable's earthy cynicism.

Shortly before the outbreak of the Second World War, Howard returned to England to make patriotic films and became strongly identified with the British war effort, making his last film, *The First Of The Few*, 1942, with David Niven. He was killed in June 1943, returning from a government-sponsored lecture tour of Spain and Portugal, when the plane he was in was shot down by German fighters, a moment when the shining integrity of his persona overlapped with reality.

RIGHT: *A Free Soul*, 1931, with Norma Shearer
BELOW: *The Petrified Forest*, 1936, with Bette Davis
OPPOSITE: publicity portrait for *Gone with the Wind*, 1939

DAVID NIVEN

Superbly tailored and impeccably mannered and witty, Niven also had a raffish and slightly spivvy quality that made him very naughty and sexy. He was perfectly captured as Phileas Fogg, the upper-crust man-about-town who journeys the globe for a bet in *Around The World In Eighty Days*, 1956, and who emerges from the ghastliest difficulties with barely a crease on his shirt.

Classified as Anglo-Saxon Type Number 2008, Niven strolled into a Hollywood career in 1934 as an extra in *Mutiny On The Bounty*, and went on to show a stiff upper lip for every occasion, from the horrors of war to the hurly-burly of the seduction couch; his role as the middle-aged roué who used words like 'virgin' and 'mistress' in *The Moon Is Blue*, 1953, brought him a certain spicy notoriety (the film was condemned by the Legion of Decency). Most of his films were pretty poor, though in *A Matter of Life and Death*, 1946, he was very good as an RAF officer who tries to cheat death for love, and in 1958 he won an Academy Award as the bogus major in *Separate Tables*. He was also Jean Seberg's charming *lupe* of a *père* in *Bonjour Tristesse*. In the sixties he was one of the cliff-clambering heroes of *The Guns of Navarone* and the most urbane of burglars in *The Pink Panther*. Niven published two excellent and suitably racy autobiographies, 'The Moon's A Balloon' and 'Bring On The Empty Horses', before his death from a wasting disease.

LEFT: publicity portrait for *Raffles*, 1940

Olivier's awesome theatrical presence and genius has always rooted him firmly on the stage. Before the Second World War he enjoyed romantic stardom as a classic leading man, full of dark, unresolved ambiguities about sexual passions, violence and tortured memories, notably the wild, agonized Heathcliff of *Wuthering Heights*, 1939, and the enigmatic, cultured widower who marries Joan Fontaine in *Rebecca*, 1940. More flippantly he was the snobbishly gorgeous Mr Darcy in *Pride and Prejudice*, 1940, and introduced Hollywood to one of its great screen heroines, Vivien Leigh, who promptly became Scarlett in *Gone with the Wind*.

Although never a cinema natural, Olivier made a considerable contribution through his interpretations of demanding Shakespearian roles; his performances in *Henry V*, 1944, and *Richard III*, 1955, are both considered classics, and he won an Academy Award as actor/director of *Hamlet* in 1948, the year he received his knighthood. His other notable performances include Archie Rice in *The Entertainer*, 1960, and in *Sleuth*. Despite serious illness and declining energy he has continued to work, playing a Jewish Nazi-hunter in Ira Levin's thriller *The Boys from Brazil* in 1978, and an aristocratically dilapidated Lord Marchmain in the television production of Evelyn Waugh's 'Brideshead Revisited' at the start of the eighties.

RIGHT: studio portrait, 1940.
   Photographer Laszlo Willinger

CHARLES BOYER

ABOVE: *History Is Made At Night*, 1937, with Jean Arthur
OPPOSITE: studio portrait, c. 1939. Photographer Robert Coburn

Although Boyer was a foreign lover in the throbbing, luscious mould of Valentino and Gilbert, and created the screen image of the sexy Frenchman with eyelids like a roll-top desk and a beautiful, toe-curling voice, he was durable enough to survive changing fashions; both his image and sexual presence remained believable over nearly half a century of Gallic passion. While he could handle comedy well, as he proved in such delights as *History Is Made At Night*, 1937, it was probably his quality of passionate seriousness that made him such a long-lasting screen character.

Born in France in 1899, Boyer had become a matinée idol in his home country by his early twenties, but only achieved international heart-throb status in 1936 as Crown Prince Rudolph in *Mayerling*. Two years later, he made *Algiers* with Hedy Lamarr and went on to star opposite some of the most glamorous leading ladies in the world: goddesses like Greta Garbo and Marlene Dietrich, personalities like Lauren Bacall and Ingrid Bergman, and kittens like Brigitte Bardot and Leslie Caron. In his private life he remained devoted to his wife, the English actress Pat Paterson, throughout a long marriage, and when she died of cancer in August 1978, Boyer committed suicide by taking an overdose of barbituates.

CESAR ROMERO

GILBERT ROLAND

An immaculately dressed Latin-American idol with a caddish leer, Cesar Romero started as a dance and Broadway stage star, but left for Hollywood in 1934, and embarked on a career as a tooth-flashing, moustache-waggling but slightly self-mocking charmer. His Brooklyn accent brought him mainly gangster roles in his early films, but he developed into a stylish romantic lead, as in *The Devil is a Woman*, 1935, opposite Marlene Dietrich. His own favourite role was Cortez in *Captain From Castille*, 1947. He also starred in some reasonable musicals opposite Carmen Miranda, Alice Faye and Betty Grable before maturing into character acting and comedy. Now snowy haired, his appeal, and his grin, still remain.

BELOW: publicity portrait for *The Devil is a Woman*, 1935

Roland was another Hollywood exotic, a handsome son of an ex-bullfighter who became an overnight success at the age of twenty-two as the romantic lead in *Camille*, 1927, and went on to make a good adventure hero after the arrival of sound. Born in Mexico and christened Luis Alonso, he went to Los Angeles with his family as a teenager, took a stage name – borrowed from John Gilbert and Ruth Roland – and began as an extra. Having moved up through feature parts and enjoyed a short-lived romance with Clara Bow, he made *Camille*, survived the arrival of sound by taking elocution lessons and during the fifties made many good adventure movies, notably opposite Jane Russell.

ABOVE: studio portrait, c. 1935.
Photographer George Hurrell

ABOVE: *Blonde Venus*, 1932, with
Marlene Dietrich
OPPOSITE: *Suzy*, 1936, with Jean Harlow

The most universally appealing romantic male lead of his time, Grant himself put his finger on the secret of his attraction: 'I play myself', he once said, 'to perfection.' He sustained an extraordinary high level of performance over a career that stretched from the thirties to the sixties and although he never won an Academy Award as Best Actor, perhaps because of the deceptive ease of his performances, he undoubtedly has a claim to being one of Hollywood's greatest actors. His debonair, carefree charm, natural acting gifts and awesome sense of timing made him a master of thirties light and screwball comedy, outstandingly under the direction of Howard Hawks. Through such films his image became the essence of cultivated urban sophistication, that of the smooth and desirable American male with the right manners and the right physique, a man who would always step competently over the trip-wires of fate on his way to painlessly achieved moral growth. In the forties, however, Hitchcock took Grant's persona of the desirable bachelor as a device to obvert the less appealing qualities implied underneath. In *Suspicion* Grant was cast as a dubious playboy, frightening new wife Joan Fontaine, and in *Notorious*, as a cold, emotionally blocked figure, who practically destroys Ingrid Bergman before saving her through the ultimate recognition and acknowledgement of his own feelings.

Grant did not have a very happy childhood; his mother had a breakdown when he was nine years old and he disliked school, preferring to knock around as a general dogsbody at the Hippodrome Theatre. He ran away from home to join a travelling vaudeville show at the age of thirteen and although he was brought back, he got his father's permission to rejoin when he came of age a year later; it was after a trip to New York, and then a countrywide tour of the United States with the troupe two years later, that he became enthused with the place and decided to settle there.

By 1923, Grant was playing in musical comedies on Broadway under his christened name Archibald Leach, and eight years later, undeterred by his failure to wow talent scouts – who had told him that he was bow-legged and that his neck was too thick – he set off for the West Coast. Having landed a $400-a-week contract, he changed his name to Cary Grant (taking the christian name from one of his Broadway plays and the surname from a studio list of suitable names) and made his debut the next year, in 1932, in *This Is The Night*. He rapidly built up a solid reputation as a leading man, notably in *Blonde Venus* with Marlene Dietrich, *Suzy* with Jean Harlow, *The Awful Truth* with Irene Dunne and two films – *She Done Him Wrong* and *I'm No Angel* – with Mae West, to whom he later attributed his own mastery of comedy, saying that he learned everything from her.

In 1935 he made his first film with Katharine Hepburn, *Sylvia Scarlett*. There was a tremendous chemistry between his dry elegance and her faintly zany astringency, and later in the thirties they co-starred in the classic Howard Hawks comedy, *Bringing Up Baby*. Still working with Hawks, Grant successfully adapted to the adventure genre in *Only Angels Have*

ABOVE: *Holiday*, 1938, with Katharine Hepburn
RIGHT: *Arsenic and Old Lace*, 1944, with
    Priscilla Lane

Wings, and was also marvellous with Rosalind Russell in the role-reversal *His Girl Friday*, 1940, a remake of *The Front Page*. Paired again by George Cukor with Katharine Hepburn in the comedy of the idle rich, *The Philadelphia Story*, 1940, Grant played the part of her disrespectful ex-husband perfectly; it was a smash hit, and one of the roles for which Grant is remembered by a very wide audience.

The Hawks movies give a hint of the less pleasant aspects of Grant. Although it is usually light-hearted, the ambiguity is there: male chauvinism in *Only Angels Have Wings*, teasing malice in *His Girl Friday*, emotional stagnation in *Bringing Up Baby*. In the latter Hawks uses Grant as a desiccated academic, his dry disaffection reflected in the skeleton of the brontosaurus he is reconstructing for a museum, brought to life only by Hepburn. The suggestion is that Grant's irresistible charm masks qualities of immaturity, self-centredness, misogyny and a certain parsimony of the human spirit. By looking good, he makes others look small – and enjoys doing so.

Not long afterwards, Grant began his fruitful partnership with Alfred Hitchcock, who directed him in *Suspicion*, 1941, opposite Joan Fontaine, and *Notorious*, 1946, opposite Ingrid Bergman. Grant's other two films for Hitchcock, *To Catch a Thief* with Grace Kelly and *North by Northwest* with Eva Marie Saint, both made in the fifties, were immensely successful. Hitchcock once said that there was a great problem with *Suspicion*, because audiences could never believe in Grant as a killer; but through Grant's masterly performances in this and his later work for Hitchcock we can well see the symbiotic relationship between the smooth, competent façade and the cold, unpleasant character beneath. In *North by Northwest*, for

ABOVE: *Suspicion*, 1941, with Joan Fontaine
LEFT: *Only Angels Have Wings*, 1939, with Rita Hayworth

instance, Hitchcock takes that image — the slick, successful charmer who relies on his highly prized appeal to see him through — and by robbing him of his precious identity reduces him to total impotence, from which he can only escape by showing humility and need. It goes without saying that Grant could only evince these ambiguities by being a very great actor with complete technical command.

As Grant aged, he became even more attractive and charismatic, turning the romantic myth of his image — an almost unattainable standard of

RIGHT: studio portrait, 1940.
    Photographer Clarence Sinclair Bull
BELOW: *The Philadelphia Story*, 1940, with
    Katharine Hepburn
OPPOSITE: *Notorious*, 1946, with Ingrid Bergman

masculinity — into fact. This was an important element in the credibility and staying power of his persona with the more honest audiences of the early sixties, when he made the comedy thriller *Charade*, 1963, with Audrey Hepburn. He retired from making movies in the mid-sixties, playing an older man acting cupid to Samantha Eggar and Jim Hutton in his swansong, *Walk Don't Run*, 1966.

His first three marriages, to Virginia Cherrill, Barbara Hutton, the Woolworth heiress, and Betsy Drake, all ended fairly quickly in divorce (he has indicated that his broken adult relationships had their roots in the early loss of his mother) but he had a daughter, Jennifer, at the age of sixty-two by his fourth wife, actress Dyan Cannon. He had since become a top business executive in cosmetics, making huge amounts of money. Now over eighty, he is still lean, healthy, suntanned and as sexually appealing as ever.

ABOVE: publicity portrait for *Indiscreet*, 1958
LEFT: *The Pride and the Passion*, 1957, with Sophia Loren

OPPOSITE: studio portrait, c. 1931

Stylish and witty, Melvyn Douglas was a heart-throb of thirties and forties light comedy, almost invariably taking roles as an accessory to a glamorous leading lady. His debonair personality never threatened to overwhelm his leading ladies and his unaggressive presence made him a perfect choice to stand in the shadow of most of the screen goddesses. Douglas's career had started on the stage, and it was to remain his first love, but he showed himself to be a highly skilled comedy actor in his early films. Later, after he escaped being typecast as a live dinner jacket, he gave some fine performances in character roles, winning an Oscar for his portrayal of Paul Newman's father in *Hud*, 1962.

His Hollywood career was launched in 1931 by the film version of the hit play, *Tonight or Never*, in which he recreated the lead at the request of Gloria Swanson. He continued with numerous successful comedies for different studios until the war, playing opposite Claudette Colbert in *She Married Her Boss*, 1935, Irene Dunne in *Theodora Goes Wild*, 1936, Marlene Dietrich in *Angel*, 1937, and Greta Garbo in *Ninotchka*, 1939. A few years later, he was Merle Oberon's phlegmatic husband in *That Uncertain Feeling*, 1941, and he repaired Joan Crawford's scars as the surgeon in *A Woman's Face*, 1941.

When the war came Douglas joined the army and afterwards he escaped romantic leads, giving effective performances in some more interesting roles, and returned to the stage in the fifties. He found one of his best screen roles towards the end of his career, as Gene Hackman's father in *I Never Sang For My Father*, 1970, for which he was nominated for an Academy Award.

ABOVE: *Ninotchka*, 1939, with Greta Garbo

Donat managed to spend most of his time on screen in *The Thirty-Nine Steps* handcuffed to his leading lady, yet he still managed to convey the subtler emotions as well as the light-hearted charm of the part – a measure of his personality and acting skill. Although he never fulfilled the promise of his early career, completing only nineteen films in twenty-six years, and turning down many major roles due to his asthma, those he did make were often classics and he was much loved both in Britain and in America.

Like Ronald Colman, Donat epitomised all things English and gentlemanly. Originally a stage actor, his finest asset was his beautiful voice, but he also had great screen qualities which were quickly recognised when he moved into films at the beginning of the thirties; his physical vulnerability seemed to be transmuted into an exceptionally sensitive screen persona. He first won international acclaim in Alexander Korda's *The Private Life of Henry VIII*, 1933, but his most famous performances were as the intrepid Richard Hannay in Hitchcock's *The Thirty-Nine Steps*, the sentimental but lovable schoolmaster in *Goodbye, Mr Chips*, 1939, for which he won an Oscar, and the young doctor who grows emotionally through tragedy in *The Citadel*, 1938. After the war, in 1948, he played the eloquent barrister defending *The Winslow Boy*.

During the fifties, Donat's career became blighted by ill-health and his frailty was clearly visible in his poignant last speech as the Chinese Mandarin in *The Inn of the Sixth Happiness*: 'We shall not see each other again, I think.' He died, aged fifty-three, not long afterwards.

RIGHT: studio portrait, c. 1937.
  Photographer Tunbridge

FRANCHOT TONE

ROBERT YOUNG

Tone's screen career, specializing in playboy and man-about-town roles in comedy and drama, was routine rather than staggering, but his private life was packed with incident. Married four times, his mild, well-bred image was shattered when he got involved in a bar-room brawl. He was a popular American screen and stage presence in the thirties, particularly after he met Crawford while making *Today We Live*. He went on to star in numerous romantic comedies for MGM, including *Dancing Lady*, 1933 (with Crawford), *Bombshell*, 1933 (with Jean Harlow), and found a few good parts on loan – *The World Moves On*, 1934, for John Ford and Fox, and *Dangerous*, 1935, for Warners. But, by the fifties, his screen career had dwindled and he returned to the stage. He died in 1968.

BELOW: studio portrait, c. 1933.
Photographer George Hurrell

Robert Young never lost his overwhelmingly wholesome, if lightweight, image in over eighty films mostly made during the thirties and forties. Years later he was as dependable, sympathetic and reliable as ever in the television medical drama, 'Marcus Welby MD'. Competent squire of Joan Crawford in *Today We Live*, 1933, and the daft romance *The Bride Wore Red*, 1937, Young's other leading ladies included Janet Gaynor in *Carolina*, 1934, and Shirley Temple in *Stowaway*, 1936. In all of them, he was clean, smart, honest, and as sexual as a wet sock. His private life has been as healthy and wholesome as his screen persona, his own marriage lasting over 50 years.

ABOVE: studio portrait, c. 1932
OPPOSITE: *The Bride Wore Red*, 1937, with
Joan Crawford

ROBERT TAYLOR

Taylor was a perfectly proportioned piece of beefcake whose flawless, glowing handsomeness personified male strength. He had thousands of besotted female fans and became a huge box-office draw; when he sailed to England to make *A Yank At Oxford* with Vivien Leigh in 1938, thousands of women waited for him on the quay at Southampton — and a handful were unearthed from under his bed. His acting ability was decidedly modest, but he made a tremendous leading man for some of Hollywood's strongest ladies in the thirties and forties. Off-screen, however, he was a peaceful man who avoided embroilment in

OPPOSITE: studio portrait, 1936.
Photographer Ted Allan
LEFT: *Personal Property*, 1938, with Jean Harlow
BELOW: *The Gorgeous Hussy*, 1936, with Joan Crawford

shattering personal events: a docile, grateful and uncomplaining exployee, he stayed with MGM for twenty-six years. He was married twice, to Barbara Stanwyck and Ursula Thiess.

It is tempting to suggest that Taylor's popularity with strong leading ladies was due mainly to the fact that he just stood around looking beautiful and let them get on with the acting. He throbbed at Garbo in *Camille* and gazed mooningly at Jean Harlow in *Personal Property*, but there was something innocuous and docile about him. Unlike Errol Flynn, his gorgeous features were not animated by the suggestion that he was capable of being a very bad boy indeed. Taylor summed up his early career himself: 'I was awful, the world's worst actor. But I had a couple of good things going for me – I was a good-looking kid and had a good voice. So I got the breaks.'

Born Spangler Arlington Brough, he studied music at college, where he was spotted by an MGM talent scout playing the lead in the dramatic society's production of 'Journey's End'. He took up MGM's offer of a $35-a-week contract, became Robert Taylor, and launched into his heyday with the classic weepie, *Magnificent Obsession*, 1935, playing a drunken playboy who reforms and becomes selflessly devoted to Irene Dunne. He swept audiences off their feet and within a year had played opposite some of the best leading ladies: Janet Gaynor in *Small Town Girl*, Loretta Young in *Private Number*, Barbara Stanwyck in *His Brother's Wife*, Joan Crawford in *The Gorgeous Hussy* and Greta Garbo in *Camille*. Over the next few years his image became tougher. He played a prize-fighter opposite Maureen O'Sullivan in *The Crowd Roars*, 1938, and a once-rich boy forced to work, and fight, for his living in *Stand Up and Fight*, 1939. By then he had been paired with Vivien Leigh

OPPOSITE: studio portrait, 1936.
Photographer Frank Grimes
RIGHT: *Camille*, 1937, with Greta Garbo

for the first time in *A Yank At Oxford* and two years later they came together again for his own favourite movie, the weepie *Waterloo Bridge* in which she is a ballerina forced to take to the streets and he is a dashing officer who is her unsuspecting lover. As he himself commented, 'I was never a good actor, I guess, but they sure put me in some good movies'.

Like many of his contemporaries, Taylor did not find it easy to pick up his career after the war, during which he had spent two years as a flying instructor and narrated *The Fighting Lady*, an award-winning documentary about a warship. But MGM remembered his loyalty and managed to find him roles in some classy films: *Quo Vadis*, 1951, in which he played a Roman centurion in love with a Christian, Deborah Kerr, sustained his reputation, and he followed up with more costume movies, most memorably *Ivanhoe* – made in 1952, the same year he and Barbara Stanwyck were divorced – and *The Knights of the Round Table*, 1954, in which he played Lancelot. He also made some reasonable Westerns. In 1959, he finally broke with MGM to go freelance, played for several years in the television series, 'The Detectives', and made a handful of not very memorable films before he died in 1969.

ABOVE: *Lucky Night*, 1939, with Myrna Loy
RIGHT: *Johnny Eager*, 1942, with Lana Turner
OPPOSITE: *Undercurrent*, 1946, with
      Katharine Hepburn

THE WAR YEARS

With hindsight, the war years saw the start of the erosion of Hollywood's power, and of all the things it took for granted. The world that went to the movies by the time the fifties were getting under way was a very different one from that at the end of the thirties, with East and West estranged, the British Empire disintegrating, and an impoverished Europe which was struggling to rebuild itself ideologically, sociologically and artistically.

Hollywood's war meant the adaptation of the established genres. Action pictures became battle movies and leading men became service men: Errol Flynn in *Dive Bomber*, Robert Taylor in *Flight Command* and Ray Milland in *I Wanted Wings*. They were sexy, brave and beautiful. Their counterparts, the gangsters, metamorphosed into German spies. At first, Hollywood made a rather tentative entry into the conflict, paralleling the national policy of sympathy but non-involvement. The war was treated lightly, as in Tyrone Power's film *A Yank in the R.A.F.*, or touched on allegorically, as in Errol Flynn's swashbuckling *The Sea Hawk*, rousing England to defeat the Spanish Armada – or Luftwaffe. In *Sergeant York*, Gary Cooper played a pacifist who became a World War One hero after deciding that, under certain circumstances, killing could be interpreted as doing God's work.

True involvement happened only after Pearl Harbor, when America and Hollywood entered with a vengeance. Tyrone Power, Clark Gable and Jimmy Stewart, together with most of the major male stars, were fighting and flying and doing their bit alongside the people who had paid to watch their movies. It was an age of propaganda, documentaries and morale boosters, with Hollywood backing Uncle Sam all the way.

And, as usual, there were lavish doses of fantasy. By 1946, the industry was enjoying the most lucrative period in history. The war had driven people into the cinema to escape, and the return to peace lured them there to celebrate.

What went wrong? For a start, the supply of handsome young men had diminished. In the thirties they had queued in their thousands to try to get a break in the movie business, but a decade later that was no longer true. Furthermore, the studios seemed to misunderstand the mood and climate of the times. Many of the new stars who emerged came out of old moulds and seemed out of place in a post-war world in which old assumptions no longer rang true; happy endings were no longer satisfying, and it was recognized that the good guy did not always get the breaks. It was the era of Dana Andrews, the innocent victim of a lynch-mob in *The Ox-Bow Incident*, of Alan Ladd, calm, slim and vicious, the first American actor to appear as an angelic killer, and of John Garfield, the first of the ugly-beautiful leading men.

Many of the stars of the thirties and forties had changed too. Older, sadder and wiser with a war behind them, their careers sometimes petered out – like that of Clive Brook – or, more often, foundered because they were now middle-aged men who were not really too sure that they ought to be playing romantic young heroes any more. But the studios persisted: in Clark Gable's first post-war film, *Adventure*, he was paired with Greer Garson under the slogan, 'Gable's back and Garson's got him'. The slogan made him cringe, and friends say that Greer Garson was one of the only two women that Gable truly disliked – the other was Jeanette MacDonald. And he hated the finished movie.

No wonder it bombed. Gable went on to make better films than that during his post-war career, but it was despite Hollywood's insensitivity and tendency to hark back to past glories rather than looking ahead to establish new heroes.

Significantly, the faltering of the leading man was paralleled by the growing strength of the leading lady. Rita Hayworth, Betty Grable and Lana Turner had the power that their opposite numbers were starting to lack: in part it was chance and in part the roles they were given, but also leading men were beginning to be viewed in a new light, like William Holden's gigolo/heel in *Sunset Boulevard*, 1950.

Another factor was at work in this period. In 1947, the House Un-American Activities Committee started its attack. Talent and creativity that could have seen the industry through a critical period in its history began to be driven out by a public jingoism that discredited Hollywood in the eyes of the world. Careers and lives were destroyed: John Garfield, who remained loyal to the left-wing colleagues of his early career, reacted badly to ostracism and neglect and his premature death was blamed on the treatment he had received.

The news was not all bad. Disillusionment and subversion found covert expression, often in the *film-noir* style which, after John Huston's *The Maltese Falcon*, became the dominant mode for detective films of the forties. A new type of hero — on the side of good, but not necessarily of the law — achieved a particularly potent representation in the figure of the private eye who, neither gangster nor cop, went down the mean streets immortalized by Raymond Chandler and Dashiell Hammett. Humphrey Bogart projected the ambivalence perfectly. He became one of the most powerful male figures of the screen: the hero stripped of fake 'goody' attributes and values irrelevant to current mores. A loner and romantic figure, he was very much his own man, concealed emotion behind a cynical exterior; in *High Sierra* and *The Maltese Falcon* he was playing 'tough guys' whose redeeming quality was a strict moral code, a type whose influence can be traced through to Clint Eastwood and Nick Nolte. Like Gable, Grant and Cooper before him, Bogart was liked by men as well as women; unlike them, he was attractive without being a conventional specimen of male beauty. It signalled a fundamental change in the types who were acceptable, and therefore came to be cast, as leading men.

Across thousands of miles of land and water, Jean Gabin, the greatest star the French cinema ever had, was developing an image on remarkably similar lines. English audiences, however, were being fed frothy post-war comedies of the high life in which the bootboy in-love-with-M'Lady always turned out to be heir to a dukedom in disguise, and debutantes danced till dawn without taking off their clothes. Their leading men were of quite a different brand, with British charm and stiff upper lip. Yet in their case too — stars like Michael Wilding and Rex Harrison — there were often hints that all was not quite as it appeared on the surface.

ERROL FLYNN

Errol Flynn was one of the most handsome and romantic leading men to come out of Hollywood. A gallant, with a graceful animal presence, his virile exploits made him the embodiment of male dreams and the object of female fantasies. His private life, however, was unruly and tragic. He lived for years on the edge of disaster and eventually fell from grace and became an object of anger and ridicule.

He came to Hollywood from the English stage, bouncing to stardom in the mid-thirties with another new face, Olivia de Havilland, in *Captain Blood*, 1935. Their magnificent chemistry made *The Charge of the Light Brigade*, 1936, *The Adventures of Robin Hood*, 1938, and *They Died With*

OPPOSITE: portrait, c. 1939
LEFT: *The Adventures of Robin Hood*, 1938, with Olivia De Havilland
BELOW: portrait, c. 1935

Their Boots On, 1941, enormous box-office successes. Like Doug Fairbanks Sr, his guiding principle as a leading man was never to settle for taking a lady out to dinner when he could be scaling a castle wall to rescue her from the Sheriff of Nottingham. These were Flynn's golden years when he was a giant star and the darling of Hollywood with an adoring public, studio and press. He starred in *The Dawn Patrol* with David Niven, matched Bette Davis in *The Private Lives of Elizabeth and Essex*, 1939, tamed the West in *Dodge City* and swashbuckled in *The Sea Hawk*; always in the role of the brave, manly hero who was not fully dressed without a sword between his teeth or a longbow in his hand.

Flynn's early life was as adventurous as that depicted in any of his films. Born in Tasmania, the son of a marine biologist, he had an unhappy relationship with his mother and took off for Papua New Guinea at the age of seventeen, having been expelled from numerous institutes of learning. There he tried his hand at gold mining, managed a tobacco plantation and worked as a patrol officer, smoking opium and fighting Japanese in China along the way.

Soon afterwards, Flynn married the French actress Lili Damita. Far from a model husband, and with a reputation as a stud, his exploits were laughed off until the end of 1942, when he was charged with having sex with two under-age girls. The court case destroyed him, despite the fact that he was acquitted. He divorced Lili, remarried and fathered two girls, then divorced again and married Patrice Wymore in 1950. In the meantime, though he continued to appear in major films, notably *The Sun Also Rises*, 1957, his popularity had flagged. He drank a great deal, had a last fling with a teenage girlfriend, and died in 1959.

ABOVE: *Dodge City*, 1939, with
    Olivia De Havilland
RIGHT: *Against All Flags*, 1946, with
    Maureen O'Hara

Alan Ladd could never understand his own popularity; only 5ft 6in tall, he had to stand on boxes to meet other actors in the eye, and he once described his build as that of an undernourished featherweight. But he was also extremely handsome with an air of downbeat, withdrawn violence and a look of psychological suffering that made him equally attractive as a taciturn, vulnerable good or bad guy. Ladd became a star overnight after his portrayal of the fair, trench-coated killer in *This Gun for Hire* in 1942, and stayed on top for twenty years despite a relative dearth of good films. His most memorable part was in the epic Western *Shane*, which used Ladd's screen image to suggest the covert ruthlessness that made the character believable.

The son of an accountant who died when he was three, Ladd had grown up in California during the Depression, taken various odd jobs, and worked as an extra and a technician before honing his distinctive voice on radio and marrying his agent, Sue Carol. The film parts began to come in and after the success of his casting opposite Veronica Lake in *This Gun for Hire*, they were teamed up again for *The Glass Key*, 1942, and *The Blue Dahlia*, 1946, both good little-guy thrillers. Well after the peak of his career came *Shane* in 1953, but it was an epic performance, with Ladd as the gunfighter trying to give up his trade, but forced to kill in order to save the lives of others. Ladd later refused the offer of the James Dean role in *Giant*, and towards the end of the fifties he lost his looks, drank heavily and made largely unremembered films, dying at the age of fifty-one from an overdose of sedatives mixed with alcohol.

RIGHT: publicity portrait for *This Gun for Hire*,
1942, with Veronica Lake

JOSEPH COTTEN

Cotten was already a distinguished theatrical actor when he came to the screen as a protégé of Orson Welles. He brought out Cotten's hard-bitten, cynical edge in *Citizen Kane*, 1941, and exploited his tough, quiet authority in *The Magnificent Ambersons* and *Journey Into Fear*, both 1942, before casting him as the writer who hunts Harry Lime through the zither-filled streets of Vienna in *The Third Man*.

Hitchcock saw a tortured quality behind Cotten's romantic façade, casting him as an ex-convict married to dipsomaniac Ingrid Bergman in *Under Capricorn*, 1949, and as the smart, handsome murderer with a pathological hatred of old women in *Shadow of a Doubt*, 1943, where Cotten transmits a strong sense of sexual disgust. Other good performances were as the noble brother of bad guy Gregory Peck in *Duel in the Sun* and the struggling portrait artist in love with Jennifer Jones in *Portrait of Jennie*, for which he won the Best Actor award in the Venice Festival in 1948. His career has been less splendid since; from Marilyn Monroe's husband in *Niagara*, 1953, and other portraits of hen-pecked middle-age, to a surgeon pursued by Vincent Price in *The Abominable Dr Phibes*, 1971. Orson Welles got him to appear, uncredited, as the drunken coroner in *Touch of Evil*, 1958.

LEFT: studio portrait, c. 1944.
Photographer John Miehle

Ray Milland established himself as a pleasant, smiling, romantic lead in the late thirties, but by the next decade he had developed the darker and more interesting persona revealed in Billy Wilder's *The Lost Weekend*, 1945, as the searingly self-destructive alcoholic. Welsh by birth, and christened Reginald Truscott-Jones, he started off in British films at the end of the twenties, made his Hollywood debut as Spike Milland, switched his name again and quickly graduated to romantic lead status. He played an English lord opposite Claudette Colbert in *The Gilded Lily*, 1935, a tycoon's son in *Easy Living*, 1937, and a rich playboy in *I Wanted Wings*, 1941.

Wilder cast him in a less straightforward role in *The Major and the Minor*, 1942, in which he is worriedly attracted to Ginger Rogers disguised as a pre-teen. Milland continued to find interesting roles: with Ginger Rogers again in *Lady in the Dark*, 1944; as a fop helping Paulette Goddard into polite society in *Kitty*, 1945; and as the British officer helped out of Nazi Germany by Marlene Dietrich in *Golden Earrings*, 1947.

In his fifties he moved off in a new direction, acting in, and sometimes directing, several very good low-budget movies – *The Man with the X-Ray Eyes*, *Panic In Year Zero!* and *The Thing with Two Heads*. He was given one of his best later roles, cast against type, as the charming ex-tennis star organising the murder of his wife, Grace Kelly, in Hitchcock's *Dial M for Murder*, 1954. More recently – and most would say less notably – he played Ryan O'Neal's father in *Love Story*, 1970, and has aged gracefully into character acting for both Hollywood and television blockbusters.

ABOVE: *Easy Living*, 1937, with Jean Arthur

HUMPHREY BOGART

The essential Bogart has always been Rick, the expatriate café-owner of *Casablanca*; wounded but still stirred by Ingrid Bergman, he ultimately decides to place honour and self-possession above passion. In that role he became the blueprint of one of the screen's most powerful symbols of masculinity – the intelligent, sardonic man on the edge of conventional society, who pursues his own rigid code of principle and honour and rarely lowers his emotional guard because he foresees the chaos of letting go. In the early sixties, *Casablanca* was to become a cult movie and Bogart a cult hero. Bogie addicts, most of them too young to have seen the movie when it first came out, knew every single classic line: 'Here's looking at you, kid.' 'We'll always have Paris.' 'The problems of three little people don't amount to a hill o' beans in this crazy world.' It was an era of man-made evils – cold war, assassination, corruption, pollution – and the new generation was looking back for inspiration to the cynical, pessimistic hero of a piece of five-star romance.

Bogart was short and stocky, and was not a conventionally good-looking male: 'How can an ugly man be so handsome?' asked Marta Toren in *Sirocco*. Indeed Warners could not conceive of him as a heart-throb at all and for much of his career in the thirties, they projected only his tough-guy persona. He later claimed that of his first thirty-four pictures, he was shot in twelve, electrocuted or hanged in eight, and a jailbird in nine. Like Cagney he had an inimitable style of delivery perfectly suited to gangster roles; he spoke as though he were munching iron filings, with a faint and much imitated lisp. But his vulnerable toughness, detached chivalry and tantalizing blend of distance and intimacy also made him one of the great romantic heroes.

OPPOSITE: studio portrait, c. 1939
ABOVE: *A Devil With Women*, 1930, with Mona Maris
LEFT: *High Sierra*, 1941, with Ida Lupino

115

Bogart had carved out a career as a romantic juvenile in the theatre, but was taken off to the West Coast by Fox, with whom he had made a handful of pictures, including *Up the River* in 1930, which marked the start of a lifelong friendship with its star, Spencer Tracy. However, Bogart was dropped by Fox and it was only in 1936, when Leslie Howard prevailed upon Warner Brothers to use Bogart (rather than Edward G. Robinson) for the screen role of Duke Mantee in *The Petrified Forest*, on the strength of his stage performance, that he established himself in Hollywood. His success won him a place in Warners' stable of gangsters and he appeared in a series of tough-guy films, of which the best were *San Quentin*, 1937, and Raoul Walsh's *They Drive by Night*, 1940.

Over the next five years, Bogart made some of his classic films. In 1941, he played the lonely, detached outsider in *High Sierra*, and appeared as Sam Spade in *The Maltese Falcon*. In 1942, he starred as Rick in *Casablanca*. Then, in 1944, he made *To Have and Have Not*, an adaptation of the Hemingway novel which featured a newcomer named Lauren Bacall. She was only twenty, he was forty-five; but they plunged into love and he got a divorce from his third wife — a volatile blonde named Mayo Methot who had always matched him drink for drink and punch for punch — to marry Bacall. Bogart and Bacall's crackling attraction for each other was immortalized in *The Big Sleep*, 1946, and *Key Largo*, 1948. The voltage of the scenes between Bogart and Bacall raises the question whether real-life lovers make better screen pairings. Certainly all their scenes are intriguing because of the real feeling between them. On the other hand, Bogart and Bergman also made a wonderful pairing — cynical, unwilling Rick, cold, hard and introspective, opposite soft, generous Ilsa,

ABOVE: *Casablanca*, 1942, with Ingrid Bergman
RIGHT: *Across the Pacific*, 1942, with Mary Astor
OPPOSITE: *Dark Passage*, 1947, with
    Lauren Bacall

so open and vulnerable — and yet it is rumoured that Bogart was close to dislike of his co-star. But then, maybe that is what gave his final rejection of her an extra edge.

At a time when the general mood, politically as well as socially, was conservative, Bacall and Bogart were both vociferous in their support of Adlai Stevenson and the Democrats; also Bogart's private life featured some heavy drinking and well-documented pranks with Hollywood cronies. Nevertheless, he continued getting good parts and made some memorable films, notably *In a Lonely Place*, 1950, with Gloria Grahame, *The Treasure of the Sierra Madre*, 1948, *The Caine Mutiny*, 1954, and, with Katharine Hepburn, *The African Queen*, 1951, before he embarked on his battle against cancer of the oesophagus. His last film was *The Harder They Fall*, 1956, and he died in January 1957.

OPPOSITE: studio portrait, 1946.
    Photographer Bert Six
RIGHT: *Dead Reckoning*, 1947, with
    Lizabeth Scott

SPENCER TRACY

Spencer Tracy first appeared – on Broadway – as a robot, but graduated to respected eminence playing flawed though fundamentally good characters; men of strength and integrity who represented American normality. Craggy and dignified but also sharp-tongued, he was the son of a truck salesman and had originally intended to go into the priesthood, and his casting in some of his most memorable roles turned on his sense of Catholic integrity. He once said his face was 'as plain as a barn door' but thanks to his on/off screen pairing with Hepburn, he also had a strong romantic image.

Tracy made his film debut for John Ford in *Up the River* in 1930, and although he was successful for Fox, he

was not the most pliant of actors and was sacked in 1935. Promptly signed by MGM, he made two outstanding films in the next few years, winning two Oscars: the first in 1937 for *Captains Courageous* and the second the following year for his performance as Father Flanagan, reforming Mickey Rooney in *Boys Town*.

His glorious screen partnership with Katharine Hepburn began in *Woman of the Year*, 1942, and they went on to make wonderful comedies, playing with the notion of contest between masculine and feminine wiles. One of the best examples was as the married lawyers in *Adam's Rib*, a film which gave a very representative view of masculinity in the forties, in which either of the sexes may outsmart each

other, but the man is always on top in the bedroom. Off screen, Tracy had a lifelong romantic friendship with Hepburn, but he never divorced his wife, Louise Treadwell, and the relationship was treated discreetly by the gossip columnists of the day. Tracy emerged from the retirement caused by his poor health, to make *Guess Who's Coming to Dinner* in 1967 with Hepburn; although obviously extremely ill, he carried on working on the production and died only shortly after its completion.

ABOVE: *Woman of the Year*, 1942, with Katharine Hepburn
OPPOSITE: publicity portrait, c. 1931

DANA ANDREWS

A decent, all-American type whose good looks could convey a certain shiftiness or insecurity, Dana Andrews came rather late to movies: he had trained as a singer and qualified as an accountant before Sam Goldwyn signed him at the end of the thirties. He graduated to leading-man status during the war and adapted well to playing the uneasier heroes of the post-war years. Significantly, they were often good guys who got bad breaks: strung up as the innocent scapegoat of a lynch mob in *The Ox-Bow Incident*, 1943; the love-stricken detective in Preminger's *Laura*, 1944; driven to drink in *The Best Years of Our Lives*, 1946; and 'framed' for murder in *Beyond A Reasonable Doubt*, 1956.

ABOVE: publicity portrait for *The Purple Heart*, 1944

GLENN FORD

Usually thought of as an amiable but strong hero, with suitably clenched teeth and a quietly threatening voice, Glenn Ford steamed to fame in a brilliantly tormented performance opposite Rita Hayworth in *Gilda* in 1946. Ford had worked on stage in the thirties and appeared in a string of 'B' movies, then served as a marine before starring opposite Bette Davis in *A Stolen Life*, 1946. Off screen, he played leading man to Judy Garland, Angie Dickinson and Hope Lange, and married Eleanor Powell in 1943.

Ford's versatility is shown by his fine performances as the pathological cop avenging his wife's murder in Fritz Lang's *The Big Heat*, 1953, the schoolmaster in *The Blackboard Jungle*, 1955, and the American captain in *The Teahouse of the August Moon*, 1956.

BELOW: *Affair In Trinidad*, 1952, with Rita Hayworth

An ugly-beautiful forerunner of Brando and James Dean, Garfield played tough, cynical street punks pushed into crime by society; he exuded a very troubled sexuality which for the first time was acceptable for a star with mass sexual appeal. His real life closely resembled the persona: born Julius Garfinkel in New York, his mother died when he was seven and, since his father found it difficult to control him, he was billeted with a succession of relatives, but spent most of his time on the street. After winning a scholarship to the Ouspenskaya Drama School, he formed a life-long friendship with playwright Clifford Odets, became associated with the left-wing Group Theatre and attracted notice first of all in Odets's play 'Awake and Sing'. Garfield's political loyalties were later to prove his undoing; after refusing to give names to the House Un-American Activities Committee in the early fifties, he was to find it very difficult to get work.

Garfield packed a lot into his short, rebellious and scandalous life. His best movies included the steamy *The Postman Always Rings Twice*, 1946, opposite Lana Turner, and in the following year *Humoresque*, as Joan Crawford's lover, and *Body and Soul* as a boxer. In *Force of Evil*, 1948, he gave an extraordinary performance as an attorney involved in a numbers racket. Meanwhile, his private life featured lots of drinking and smoking, a first heart attack at thirty-six, and numerous affairs and sexual escapades. His last good starring role was in *The Breaking Point*, 1950, a remake of *To Have and Have Not*, and two years later he died of a heart attack, aged only thirty-nine, in the company of a starlet.

ABOVE: publicity portrait for *We Were Strangers*, 1949

MICHAEL WILDING

REX HARRISON

Michael Wilding was a dashing, charming, well-cut sort of chap, one of the most popular heroes of the British screen in the late forties, when a stiff upper lip was an essential qualification for a leading man. Son of an army officer and an actress, Wilding started out as a commercial artist and arrived in films through the art department of a British studio. A member of the crew in Noël Coward's navy yarn *In Which We Serve*, 1942, he was later a natural for frothy post-war confections like *Spring in Park Lane*, 1948, playing Anna Neagle's lackey who turns out to be a young aristocrat, and *The Glass Slipper*, 1955, in which he was Leslie Caron's Prince Charming. He also won fame in the USA for being one of Elizabeth Taylor's husbands.

BELOW: publicity portrait for *Piccadilly Incident*, 1946, with Anna Neagle

Rex Harrison's English gentlemen were highly sophisticated but often dishonourable. He usually appeared as a pleasant if blasé smoothie, and while Noël Coward once told him, 'After me, you're the best light comedian in the world', his lightness of manner had an edge of emotional sadism.

Harrison's international career burgeoned after the war when he went to Hollywood to star in *Anna and the King of Siam*, 1946. He won an Oscar nomination as Caesar opposite Liz Taylor in *Cleopatra*, 1963, then won the award as the British male chauvinist, Henry Higgins, in the musical *My Fair Lady*, 1964. Popularly known as Sexy Rexy, his six wives have included Lilli Palmer, Kay Kendall and Rachel Roberts.

ABOVE: publicity portrait for *The Reluctant Debutante*, 1958, with Kay Kendall

Jean Gabin made his name in the thirties in France as a tough, doomed, ugly-beautiful anti-hero, before maturing into Spencer Tracy-type roles of vigorous seniority; many of his qualities foreshadowed Belmondo and Depardieu – working-class ruggedness, honesty and integrity. He survived all the changing fashions in the cinema and, astonishingly, was still his country's most popular actor at the end of the sixties.

The son of music hall entertainers, he started work as a labourer before entering show business as a dancer with the Folies-Bergère. His first film, *Chacun Sa Chance*, 1930, was followed by fine performances over the next decade in classics of the French cinema like *Pépé le Moko*, playing a Parisian king of crime who comes out for love of a woman and is slaughtered by police, and *La Grande Illusion*, in which he was a working-class officer in a First World War prison camp. In 1939 he made *Le Jour Se Lève*, playing a factory worker who, with justification, kills lecher Jules Berry and then waits in a hotel room for the police to come and get him.

A year later, Gabin decided to try his luck in Hollywood but he did not trans-plant successfully and returned to Europe to fight with the Free French. His forties and fifties pictures with such directors as Carné, Becker and Renoir, were consistently good and in 1958 he played Simenon's inspector hero for the first time in *Maigret Tend Un Piège*. By the time he died in 1976, he had become a national institution.

ABOVE: *La Bête Humaine*, 1938, with Simone Simon

PAUL HENREID

ABOVE: *Now Voyager*, 1942, with Bette Davis

OPPOSITE: studio portrait, 1938.
Photographer Laszlo Willinger

Typically well-bred and gallant, Paul Henreid managed to win the sympathy of the audience in *Casablanca*, despite all the pain he caused Humphrey Bogart, as the resistance hero married to Ingrid Bergman. His other famous performance was in *Now Voyager*, 1942, opposite Bette Davis. Like other Europeans — Boyer and Colman — he was seen by the Americans as a repository of good manners, and most of his other appearances, though less inspiring, were also as elegant continental lovers.

The son of a wealthy Viennese banker, born in Trieste while it was still Austrian, Henreid had started out in publishing before he became a star of Max Reinhardt's Vienna theatre. He then went to England to work on stage and in film and left for Hollywood at the start of the forties. He became an American citizen, spent the next few years as a romantic support and when his appeal faded in the fifties, he moved into film and television direction. His most notable effort was in *Dead Ringer*, 1964, in which he was caught in the middle of twin Bette Davises.

reader in the *film noir Nightmare Alley*, 1947, but failed to escape his pre-war mould and returned to staightforward adventure heroes in various genres. However, in Billy Wilder's courtroom drama, *Witness for the Prosecution*, 1958, he played a man on trial for murdering Norma Varden, with only one witness – wife Marlene Dietrich –

able to provide an alibi. The same year he died after a heart attack on set; in suitably heroic style he had been duelling with George Sanders during the filming of *Solomon and Sheba*. Tragically, three months after his death, his wife, Linda Christian, gave birth to the son he had so desperately wanted.

OPPOSITE ABOVE: *Blood and Sand*, 1941, with Rita Hayworth
OPPOSITE BELOW: *Ladies in Love*, 1936, with Loretta Young
ABOVE: *The Black Swan*, 1942

THE FIFTIES

For the cinema, the fifties was a decade of crisis and renewal. The power of the studios continued to decline; their monopoly system was destroyed by anti-trust laws which removed their control over the final product. Yet their expectations remained unrealistically high. The McCarthy anti-communist witch-hunts continued, robbing Hollywood of both creative and original talents and its credibility. Some outcasts never worked again, while others went on to Europe and their vigour helped a cinema revival to burgeon.

The breakdown of the studio system meant that the whole superstar machine was grinding down. The forties had produced fewer leading men of lasting impact and the gods of the thirties could no longer be realistically seen as throbbing romantic leads. The raw material for new stars was still there, but by the end of the fifties it was no longer necessarily heading for Hollywood; talent was neither docile nor motivated enough to allow the studios to mould and cosmetisize, then package it to maximum advantage. And even when the talent was available, Hollywood was not necessarily geared to watch over every last detail of a contract professional's public and private life.

While all this was going on, television was taking off as a popular medium. You can imagine the panic on the West Coast. Having already lost European markets as a result of the Second World War, they now discovered that previously captive audiences were staying in to watch 'I Love Lucy'. The American cinema figured out that the answer to the small black-and-white screen was the big screen and colour. Much of the technology had been around since the twenties, but only now was it seen as the cure for the ills of an ailing industry. Hence the fifties became an era of technical razzmatazz —

Cinerama, CinemaScope, Todd-AO and 3-D — to try and impress audiences and sweep them along in an overwhelming physical involvement. Clearly, these innovations lent more to certain types of films than others: above all, epic entertainment, historical, biblical and Western, from *The Robe* and *Quo Vadis* through to *The Big Country* and, later on, *Ben-Hur* and *Spartacus*. Some wonderful musicals were produced, like *Singin' in the Rain*, one of the finest to come out of Hollywood. In other words, as a slogan of the time, read 'Big Screens mean Big Themes'. This translated into the need for a different kind of leading man who could, as a primary qualification, quite simply dominate all that cinematic acreage. Charlton Heston was the most physically imposing and able of them all as Judah Ben-Hur, for example, pitting his white horses against Messala's blacks in the agonizingly exciting chariot race. Kirk Douglas's energy and magnetism dominated every part he played, from boxer Midge Kelly in *Champion*, who dies from his ring injuries rather than accept defeat, to *Spartacus*, the gladiator, eyes gleaming as metallically as his sword. Burt Lancaster, who had yet to show his depths as an actor, swung between the masts in *The Crimson Pirate* — 'Believe all that you see! No, believe only half what you see!' Robert Mitchum was already far more than a hulk; his career survived a dope bust in 1948 — the public assumed it was just another scene from one of his movies — brought the anti-hero up to date and paved the way for a new generation of wise-cracking tough guys.

Meanwhile, as the fifties progressed and the younger generation increasingly had money in its pockets, it acquired its own heroes and its own culture — rock-and-roll. Instead of plugging on regardless in the grand old manner, the studios were forced to take notice and borrow. It began with the raw excitement and violence of *Rock Around the Clock*, but became an era of teen-idols, insipid blond hunks, muscly surfers and pin-up boys like Tab Hunter, Troy Donahue and Frankie Avalon, who would lure the kids into the drive-in where they spent most of their time kissing in the back seat, but kept half an eye on the film in case their moms quizzed them when they got home. It was in the music, it was in the air.

By far the most important development of the late fifties, in terms of the emergence of a new kind of leading man, was the development of a new kind of actor. Marlon Brando, Montgomery Clift and James Dean, and later Paul Newman and Steve McQueen, had all studied at Lee Strasberg's Actors' Studio in New York, the centre of method acting and naturalism. They started off in the theatre at a time when it was being revitalized with fresh ideas and talents — for instance the work of Tennessee Williams — and they transferred their working-class protagonist roles to the screen. There was a new style: they muttered and were inaudible, prepared meticulously for their parts and explored different acting techniques. Even more important, they played their characters as men with emotional problems and flaws, rather than straight-forwardly good figures — think of Brando in a sweat-stained T-shirt, raping Vivien Leigh in *A Streetcar Named Desire*, James Dean racing a stolen car to the cliff edge in *Rebel Without a Cause*, or tortured Montgomery Clift prepared to murder his girlfriend for the sake of Elizabeth Taylor in *A Place in the Sun*. Here were leading men who at last acted out the clearly visible realities of everyday life.

BURT LANCASTER

Legend has it that Lancaster was discovered in an elevator by a stage producer who thought he was an actor and invited him to read for a Broadway part. He not only got the part, but also lasted long enough in the role to be spotted by Hollywood talent scouts. A graceful, swaggering chunk of a man whose compelling physical presence is combined with intriguing tenderness, he grew up on Manhattan's rough East Harlem area and won an athletics scholarship to college, but left to become a circus acrobat. In his first movie, *The Killers*, 1946, he was a hunk in an undershirt waiting for his killers; it made him a major star and he went on to appear in some notable fun thrillers, including the swashbuckling *The Crimson Pirate*, 1952

Other major films include *From Here to Eternity*, 1953, *Sweet Smell of Success*, 1957, and *The Birdman of Alcatraz*, for which he won a Venice Festival award in 1962. But he has also come to be appreciated as an extremely sensitive actor. He won an Oscar for *Elmer Gantry*, 1960, and displayed intriguing tenderness and a forceful sense of oppressed power and passion in two electrifying performances for Visconti; first in *The Leopard*, 1963, and then as an aging professor confronting homosexuality in *Conversation Piece*, 1974.

One of the first modern actors to set up a production company, he still appears in major films, although increasingly in character roles, still as strapping and vital as ever.

OPPOSITE: publicity portrait for *The Killers*, 1946
ABOVE: *Criss Cross*, 1948, with Yvonne de Carlo

KIRK DOUGLAS

Douglas's screen persona is that of the driven man: a self-centred, volcanic and relentless spirit reflected in extraordinarily cold, fierce eyes. That persona found perfect expression in his finest performance – the part of Dax, the First World War officer in Kubrick's *Paths of Glory*, 1957, who takes on the corrupt bureaucracy of the army in order to try and secure justice for a unit court-martialled for mutiny. In both *The Bad and the Beautiful*, 1952, and *Out of the Past*, 1947, he became a more unorthodox kind of hero – a supreme egotist who will do anything to get what he wants.

Although Douglas's image is that of the virile American, he was in fact the son of Russian immigrants and made it the hard way, putting himself through university and drama school by working as a waiter, a professional wrestler and a bell-hop. He made his Broadway debut in 1941, broke off to do war service in the navy, then made several films before hitting the jackpot in 1949 with *Champion*, playing a boxer who would K.O. his own granny to get to the top. In the fifties and sixties, he went on to make a string of exceptional films: apart from *Paths of Glory* his credits include *Ace in the Hole*, 1951, *Lust for Life*, 1956, *Spartacus*, 1960, and *Two Weeks in Another Town*, 1962.

OPPOSITE: studio portrait, 1946.
Photographer A.L. 'Whitey' Schafer
ABOVE: publicity portrait for *The Big Sky*, 1952
LEFT: *The Bad and the Beautiful*, 1952, with Lana Turner

GREGORY PECK

Peck is happier being a monument to human decency than he is as a sex symbol, and it was once said that he was 'wooden to the core'. The trouble with Peck's leading men is that since they are almost invariably required to personify such worthy characteristics as integrity, sincerity and liberal thought, he often comes through with almost no spark of life at all. But nobody could accuse him of being just a handsome bonehead in *To Kill a Mockingbird*, as Atticus Finch, a small-town lawyer defending a black man accused of rape; or as the high-principled officer in *The Guns of Navarone*, or in the early *Gentleman's Agreement*, as the journalist posing as a Jew in order to probe American anti-Semitism. While it is true that he rarely inflames us with passion, he makes his best characters vivid through the moral conflicts that nag them.

Exempt from military service through a long-standing spine injury, Peck became an almost instant war-time star in an industry deprived of many of its leading men. He had spent most of his childhood with relatives after his parents had divorced, and enrolled at the Neighborhood Play-house in New York after studying at the University of California. After work-ing on Broadway, he headed for Holly-wood in 1943 and made his debut in *Days of Glory*, 1944. In a career span-ning more than thirty years, he has brought a heavyweight presence to films of almost every genre: drama, Westerns, action and war movies, even romantic comedy. Some of them have been exceptional. His early films included *The Keys of the Kingdom*, 1945, *The Yearling*, 1946, *Gentle-man's Agreement*, 1947, and *The Gun-fighter*, 1950. However, he has also looked beyond self-sacrificing and saintly roles, as in *Duel in the Sun*, 1946, and *Moby Dick* in 1956.

OPPOSITE: studio portrait, 1945.
Photographer Ernest Bachrach
ABOVE: *Spellbound*, 1945, with Ingrid Bergman
RIGHT: *Duel in the Sun*, 1946, with
Jennifer Jones

Peck's first marriage ended in 1953; he met his second wife, Véronique, a French journalist, when she was despatched to interview him for 'Paris Match'. Now one of the grand old men of the cinema, he has served as President of the Academy of Motion Picture Arts and Sciences. He is also associated with many charitable and political causes and retains his off-screen liberal links: a few years back he discovered that he occupied a prominent position on Richard Nixon's list of dangerous enemies.

RIGHT: publicity portrait for *The Great Sinner*, 1949
BELOW: *Roman Holiday*, 1953, with Audrey Hepburn

Holden once described himself as a 'journalist of the emotions', perceptively indicating both his strengths – he proved himself capable of handling almost any type of role from comedy to adventure and almost any leading lady from Sophia Loren to Grace Kelly – and his limitations. His persona, clean-cut but with the suggestion that he was not as innocuous as he seemed, was brilliantly used by Billy Wilder in *Sunset Boulevard*, 1950, a film rich in irony about the role of the leading man. Holden, the weak male preyed upon by the female predator, played the struggling screenwriter turned gigolo to aging movie star Gloria Swanson, and the film opens with him floating in a pool like a dead fly.

Spotted at the Pasadena Playhouse by a talent scout, Holden's first proper film role was as boxer-violinist Joe Bonaparte in *Golden Boy*, 1939; it made him a star and he went on to play numerous boy-next-door types before doing Second World War service as a lieutenant in the army. His image became far harder for the psychotic killer in *The Dark Past*, 1949, and the tough, cynical hero of the prison movie *Stalag 17*, for which he won an Oscar in 1953. Around the same time, Holden also made some outstanding comedy appearances, notably in Wilder's *Sabrina*, 1954, opposite Audrey Hepburn. As he grew older his later movies – *The Bridge on the River Kwai*, 1957, *The Wild Bunch*, 1969, and *Network*, 1976 – revealed harder, more determined elements in his screen character. He died an alcoholic in 1981.

OPPOSITE: publicity portrait for *The Turning Point*, 1952
ABOVE: *Picnic*, 1955, with Kim Novak
LEFT: *The Key*, 1958, with Sophia Loren

ROBERT MITCHUM

The recent, somewhat belated, enthusiasm for *Out of the Past*, 1947, has rightly elevated Robert Mitchum to his status as one of the great movie actors. It was his classic role; the warm, wisecracking private-eye Jeff Markham, who is trying to escape a past flame, 'Nothing mattered except I had her'. A natural performer whose strong and unsmilingly humorous presence has been compared with that of Bogart, he is more rugged and stoical, less moral and vulnerable. 'You look like you're in trouble,' says a taxi-driver to private-eye Mitchum, 'because you don't look like it,' and that sums up the appealing ambiguity of Mitchum's lizard-eyed insouciance and nonchalant toughness.

As an adolescent, Mitchum got into trouble with the authorities, fleeing from a week's service on a chain gang at the age of sixteen, and by the time he drifted into acting he had worked as a nightclub bouncer, ditch-digger, professional boxer and screenwriter. He started as a heavy in a series of Hopalong Cassidy Westerns, but his big break came in *The Story of G.I. Joe*, 1945, for which he was nominated for an Oscar as Best Supporting Actor. Other outstanding films include *Pursued*, 1947, *Angel Face*, 1952, *The Night of the Hunter*, 1955, *The Sundowners*, 1960, and *Two for the Seesaw*, 1962. Married for ages, despite some sizzling affairs, he has one daughter and two sons, both of whom have become actors.

ABOVE: *Macao*, 1952, with Jane Russell
LEFT: *Out of the Past*, 1947, with Virginia Huston
OPPOSITE: publicity portrait for *Where Danger Lives*, 1950

MONTGOMERY CLIFT

Clift was one of the first modern leading men; along with Brando he brought intelligence and psychological perception to his characters. A tortured introvert who was reputedly as unhappy in private as he was on screen, he always looked slightly ill-at-ease and restless, as though he was caught unprepared. His motives were frequently at cross-purposes and his characters were nearly always ambivalent in their emotions, conveying pain and fear as well as love and desire – the flawed lover in *The Heiress*, 1949, the conscience-torn priest of Hitchcock's *I Confess*, 1953. When he was romantic it was often in a troubled way. In one of

OPPOSITE: studio portrait, c. 1949
LEFT: *The Big Lift*, 1950, with Cornell Borchers
BELOW: *Red River*, 1948, with Joanne Dru

his archetypal roles in *A Place in the Sun*, 1951, he gets his dull, small-town girl pregnant while simultaneously aiming to win rich, beautiful Elizabeth Taylor. He then plots to dispose of the obstacle to his social and financial advancement, and although he fails to carry out his plan, his girl drowns accidentally and he is sentenced to death for her murder, as if punished for his thoughts by his conscience.

Clift worked regularly on the New York stage from the age of fourteen, then made his cinema debut in 1948, for Howard Hawks in *Red River* and for Fred Zinnemann in *The Search*, for which he received an Oscar nomination. One of the first actors to suggest a conflict between the success motive and a moral sense, he was often a victim of his own impulses as in *From Here to Eternity*, 1953, in which he is brutalized by army life into committing a murder.

Off screen, Clift was an equally complicated man. Difficult to work with, he had a reputation for heavy drinking, drug abuse and disturbed behaviour. He also suffered from severe depression. In 1957 he had a terrible car accident which destroyed his dark good looks. A new insecurity in his character was exploited most fruitfully in *The Misfits*, 1961, in which he co-starred with Clark Gable and Marilyn Monroe, and in *Wild River*, 1960. His last film was *The Defector* in 1966 and shortly after it was completed he died of a heart attack.

LEFT: *Indiscretion of an American Wife*, 1952, with Jennifer Jones
OPPOSITE: publicity portrait for *A Place in the Sun*, 1951, with Elizabeth Taylor

GENE KELLY

The great moment of *Singin' in the Rain*, 1952, comes in the title number when the camera closes in on Kelly's beaming expression just as he sings, 'There's a smile on my face'. But there are other moments in the film that are nearly as good: his dreamy ballet with Cyd Charisse in the 'Broadway Rhythm' number, his hopping, jumping, flying feet in 'Moses' and the zap and humour of his movie stunts.

Kelly was not dance incarnate like Fred Astaire, but a vital, cheerful, more masculine presence who was unrivalled as a choreographer, whether in the complex set-pieces of *An American in Paris*, 1951, or in the simplicity of the rainy street set in *Singin' in the Rain*. Kelly could sing, dance, even turn his hand to straight drama and, later in his career, directed too.

Born in Pittsburgh, Kelly taught dance and dug ditches before he reached Broadway in 1938 in the chorus of the musical 'Leave it to Me'. His screen debut was in *For Me and My Gal*, 1942, opposite Judy Garland, and after that he went on to star in huge hits like *The Pirate*, 1948, opposite Garland again, *Words and Music*, 1948, doing 'Slaughter on 10th Avenue' with Vera-Ellen, and *On the Town*, 1949. In 1951 he was awarded a Special Academy Award in recognition of his versatility, 'and especially for his brilliant achievements in the art of choreography on film'.

LEFT: *Cover Girl*, 1944, with Rita Hayworth
OPPOSITE: publicity portrait for *Singin' in the Rain*, 1952

JAMES MASON

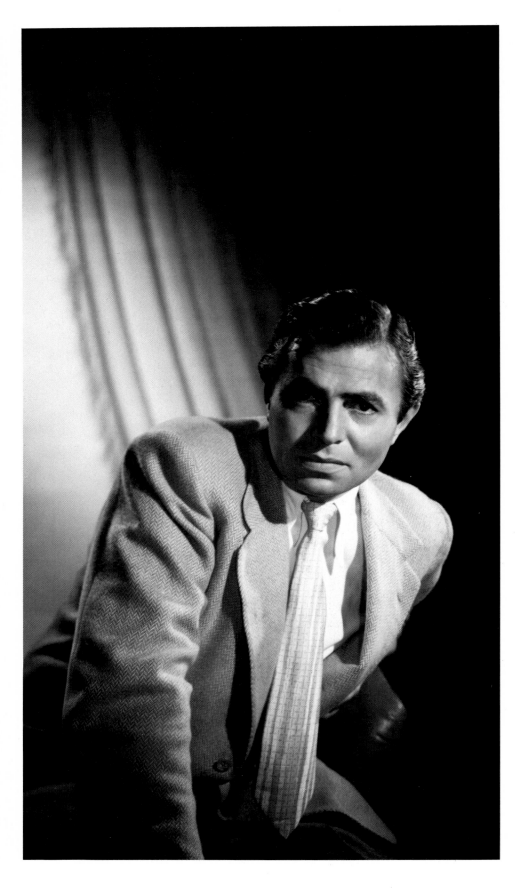

James Mason was rarely the straightforward gentleman he appeared: under the surface there usually lurked fatal flaws of weakness or cruelty, whether he was a romantic leading man, an avuncular relation or military leader. His talent — he provided Judy Garland with the best support she ever had in *A Star is Born*, 1954, and brought immense skill to the totally contrasting role of Humbert Humbert in *Lolita*, 1962 — has invariably compensated for the mediocre films which have punctuated his Hollywood career.

Born in the north of England, he went on the stage after studying architecture at Cambridge University. He then went into British films and became one of the strongest male stars by the mid-forties, notably as the sadistic Marquis, whipping Margaret Lockwood to death in *The Man in Grey*, 1943, the vicious Lord Manderstoke in *Fanny by Gaslight*, 1944, and the cruel guardian in *The Seventh Veil*, 1945. In his Hollywood films of the fifties, which were very variable, Mason often played more obviously villainous heroes; his notable performances of those years included Rommel in *The Desert Fox*, 1951, and *The Desert Rats*, 1953, the spy in *Five Fingers*, 1952, and the villain of Hitchcock's *North by Northwest*, 1959.

LEFT: studio portrait, 1950.
    Photographer Ted Reed

STEWART GRANGER

Granger's manly profile, flashing teeth and hairy chest dominated a string of rip-roaring fifties costume films, notably *Scaramouche*, 1952, *The Prisoner of Zenda*, 1952, and *Moonfleet*, 1955, as he swarthily emulated three different personas — the he-man, the Errol Flynn swashbuckler and the sexy Englishman.

Actually christened James Stewart (not the most convenient of names for an aspiring actor), he trained at drama school in England, and worked as a film extra and on the stage. He went on to become one of the top romantic attractions in British films in the forties alongside James Mason, finding his first major success in *The Man in Grey*, 1943, then in 1949 went to Hollywood and embarked on his career as an adventure hero for MGM with *King Solomon's Mines*. Seven years later, after a lot of adventure films, he became an American citizen, and, during the peak of his career, was married to actress Jean Simmons. His buccaneering style lasted until the advent of the cynical, doubt-ridden sixties, and by the seventies, when his film popularity had declined, he moved over completely to television, playing that most British of figures, the detective Sherlock Holmes in *The Hound of the Baskervilles*.

RIGHT: publicity portrait for *Scaramouche*, 1952, with Eleanor Parker

LOUIS JOURDAN

A suave, dashing continental heart-throb in the style of Charles Boyer, Jourdan is most widely remembered as Leslie Caron's pleasurable playboy lover in the musical *Gigi* in 1958 (Ze night zey invented champagne, etc). But he gave his most enduring performance ten years earlier in Max Ophüls's tormented melodrama *Letter from an Unknown Woman*, 1948, in the role of the pianist who is the undeserving object of Joan Fontaine's love; she haunts his street, he sees her and they spend the night together, but he leaves her at daybreak. The suffering he causes her is no light, half-pleasurable angst; it is appalling. Ophüls had turned Jourdan's suave, devil-may-care image on its head, just as Alfred Hitchcock had done with Cary Grant.

Jourdan trained at the Ecole Dramatique in Paris and made his French film debut in 1939 with *Le Corsaire*, then went on to play polished romantic leads in both comedy and drama until the outbreak of the Second World War when his father was arrested by the Gestapo and he joined the Resistance. After the war, David O. Selznick, producer of *Gone with the Wind*, induced him to go to Hollywood to play the lover/valet in *The Paradine Case*, 1947. His roles in the USA were straightforwardly romantic in pictures like *Madame Bovary* opposite Jennifer Jones, 1949, *Three Coins in the Fountain*, 1954, and *The Swan*, 1956, with Grace Kelly.

LEFT: publicity portrait, c. 1948

Light-hearted but soulful, Philipe was in certain ways the French James Dean of his generation: as has often been pointed out, he personified a set of ideals and attitudes, was much loved and admired, and met a tragically premature death. However, by the time he died, in his thirties, his image had shifted from the sex-preoccupied adolescent to the kind of tragi-comic hero who would later come to dominate the films of the new wave.

Born in Cannes, the son of a hotelier, he chose acting in preference to a career in medicine and in 1947 bounded to international stardom in *Le Diable au Corps* as a turbulent adolescent in love with a married woman. He became France's leading romantic film star in the post-war years, although he always continued his work in the theatre. Many of his roles in the fifties centred on the loss and pain implicit in love – *La Ronde*, 1950, *Les Grandes Manoevres*, 1955, and *Les Liaisons Dangereuses*, 1959 – and his work on the stage during those years was equally successful. In 1959, while he was working on *La Fièvre Monte à El Pao* for Buñuel, he fell ill and died afterwards of a heart attack.

ABOVE: *Le Diable au Corps*, 1947

JAMES DEAN

A week after James Dean completed his seventh film, he catapulted himself into oblivion and popular myth in his new silver Porsche: he was only twenty-four. Like Valentino and Monroe, Dean had been crystallized in a particular time by his tragic and premature death, but in his case the effect was immeasurably sharpened by his youth and the fact that his legend as the spiritual leader of a generation rests, quite uniquely, on only two movies. In both of them, *East of Eden*, 1955, and *Rebel without a*

OPPOSITE: portrait, 1955.
Photographer Sanford Roth
LEFT: portrait, c. 1954
BELOW: *Rebel without a Cause*, 1955, with Natalie Wood

Cause, 1955, he played restless, anguished heroes of burgeoning youth culture, embodying rebellion against middle-class values and hypocritical, suburban parents. As Jim in *Rebel*, he screams at his weak, indecisive, pinny-wearing father, 'I want answers now, I'm not interested in what I'll understand ten years from now'. Sulkily beautiful, he slunk around in jeans which were too tight, sneering and pouting and refusing to look adults in the eye, unloving and unlovable to them, because they either ignored him or substituted material goods for the understanding and loving acceptance he craved. His potency, though, was less in his youth than in the sadness and world-weariness he brought to his roles. Again, as Jim, when Buzz slashes his tyres, he drawls, 'You know something? You read too many comic books'. And then, when Buzz challenges Jim to a 'chicken run' and he agrees without knowing exactly what it is, except that it is dangerous, and asks his father if he should do something to save his honour, his father can tell him only not to rush into anything. The key to Dean's character was his rage and disenchantment against a world that has lost its nobility.

Dean's screen persona did not entirely have to be constructed. He had a sad, disrupted childhood himself; when he was five the family left their home in Indiana for Los Angeles, but three years later when his mother died his father sent him back to a farm in Indiana to be raised by relatives. After graduating from high school, he returned to California to attend college and began acting in a small theatre group. He made one or two television commercials, then landed bit parts in three films – *Sailor Beware*, *Fixed Bayonets* and *Has Anybody Seen My Gal* – all 1951 and 1952. Later that year he went to New York to work with the Actors' Studio and hung around the theatres, absorbing the influences that

LEFT: *East of Eden*, 1955
OPPOSITE: publicity portrait for *Giant*, 1956

turned him, like Brando, into a new kind of flawed leading man with a new acting style. Eventually he landed parts in two Broadway plays, 'See the Jaguar' and 'The Immoralist', and won the screen test with Warner which took him to Hollywood.

Dean's third major film was *Giant*, 1956, in which he had to age fifty years from a youthful wanderer to a business tycoon. The week after shooting finished, 30 September 1955, Dean crashed his car; the impact almost severed his head from his body. Ironically, his voice had only recently been heard in a road safety campaign advert, warning 'Remember, the next life you save could be mine'.

Within only a few years the Dean mythology had produced numerous books and three movies: *The James Dean Story*, 1957, and *James Dean – The First American Teenager*, 1975, and, two years later, *September 30, 1955*. His style has not dated; thirty years from his death, Matt Dillon has arrived as 'the new James Dean'.

ABOVE: *Giant*, 1956, with Elizabeth Taylor

ROCK HUDSON

A lovable, built-to-last hunk with strong box-office appeal and a broad chest that he bared to advantage, Rock Hudson was versatile enough to shine in some of Hollywood's most powerful weepies, then later, in the sixties, in fun-and-sex comedies which paired him with Doris Day. Hudson achieved success despite a lack of any formal acting training — he had worked at various jobs before making a screen career — appearing first in *Fighter Squadron* in 1948. Stardom came through director Douglas Sirk, who cast him as the hero in two powerful weepies: first in the tear-jerker *Magnificent Obsession*, 1954, opposite Jane Wyman, then in *Written on the Wind*, 1957, in which he played a man in love with married Lauren Bacall. He also carried off a demanding role opposite Elizabeth Taylor in *Giant* in 1956, becoming Hollywood's top box-office star the following year. In the sixties, Hudson developed a less conventional and somewhat camp persona, as an amiably sexy lover who was man enough to accept a successful woman, Doris Day, in the series of glamorous comedies starting with *Pillow Talk*, 1959; he also tried his luck as an adventure hero in *Ice Station Zebra*, 1968. Then, in the seventies, after several failures at the box office, he moved off into television.

RIGHT: studio portrait, 1956

TONY CURTIS

Tony Curtis's exuberant street-wise sexuality, greased D.A. haircut and tough availability made him a sensation with young audiences in the early fifties, playing knights, cowboys and cavalrymen with Bronx accents. But, in retrospect, his moment of glory was his performance in Billy Wilder's comedy *Some Like It Hot*, 1959, cross-dressing to hilarious effect and wooing Marilyn Monroe in all his butch and hairy glory.

The son of an immigrant tailor, Curtis was 'christened' Bernard Schwartz and brought up in the Bronx district of New York City, where he excelled himself in an infamous street gang. After war service in the navy, he enrolled at New York's Dramatic Workshop, found some bit parts in films, and became one of Hollywood's youngest stars in a string of Universal's swashbucklers and costume epics. In the late fifties he began to find more interesting lead roles, such as the unattractively ambitious and unprincipled press agent in *Sweet Smell of Success* which he played brilliantly, then won an Oscar nomination for *The Defiant Ones*, 1958, before discovering his flair for comedy through Billy Wilder's casting for *Some Like It Hot*. In the sixties he continued with comedy — he was both funny and attractive in *Sex and the Single Girl*, 1964 — but also moved back to serious drama, giving one of his best performances in *The Boston Strangler* in 1968.

Married three times, notably to Janet Leigh and Christine Kauffmann, his private life remains staple fodder for gossip columnists, although he has received few good roles recently.

LEFT: publicity portrait for *The Rat Race*, 1960

Elvis was the first rock idol to become a movie star, but his legendary musical fame has tended to obscure the fact that he was high amongst the top ten box-office actors for seven years, and made extremely rich men out of several film producers. Of course, producers had already got rich out of rock-and-roll films, but they had never before deigned to introduce the idols as their stars. The majority of his thirty-three films were built as vehicles for hit songs and many of them, particularly the later ones, were fairly awful; others, like *Love Me Tender*, 1956, *Jailhouse Rock*, 1957, *King Creole*, 1958, *G.I. Blues*, 1960, and *Kid Galahad*, 1962, were not at all bad, if only for their title songs. His best film as an actor was *Flaming Star*, a Western centred on the relationship between Indians and the white man, in which Presley played a half-breed. Originally conceived for Marlon Brando, the film contained almost no music at all, and its lack of big commercial success probably stopped Presley from being allowed to explore his screen talents more adventurously. Presley's raunchy style was invariably toned down to sexual inoffensiveness for the cameras and, by the close of his film career, he was down to having antiseptic friendships with girls like Mary Tyler Moore as a nun in *Change of Habit*, 1969.

RIGHT: studio portrait, c. 1959.
Photographer Virgil Apger

TAB HUNTER

Complete with crew-cut and warm, wholesome smile, Tab Hunter — That Sigh Guy — surfed in on the crest of the California look. His star movie was *Damn Yankees*, 1958, an updated musical version of 'Faust' featuring Hunter as a baseball player who literally gets rejuvenated. His brief career as a teenage rave ended when he quarrelled with Warner over the quality of his scripts and they quickly replaced him with another blond bombshell, Troy 'Parrish' Donahue, who like Hunter could not act all that well but filled out a pair of beach trunks very handsomely. Another manufactured pretty-boy star with lots of pop appeal was Frankie Avalon, whose film credits included such evocative titles as *Beach Blanket Bingo* and *How to Stuff a Wild Bikini*. Their type went out of fashion when hair grew longer and bodies got weedier. However, Hunter recently showed up in *Polyester* and *Lust in the Dust* with Divine.

ABOVE: *Battle Cry*, 1955, with Mona Freeman

MARLON BRANDO

Brando uses his body rather than his script, expressing emotion and sensuality with an extraordinary potency. Variously labelled during his early career as the Walking Hormone Factory, the Male Garbo, the Valentino of the Bop Generation and the Slob, he responded suitably by calling Hollywood 'a cultural boneyard'. Few other actors have inspired such polar reactions of critical rage and admiration, but there can be no argument that he is the most important actor of the modern cinema in America. He redrew the paradigms for leading men in the fifties and his influence can be traced to Jack Nicholson and Robert De Niro.

Brando's background was middle-class. His father was a prosperous manufacturer and his mother wrote, painted and was prominently involved in the local theatre. As a youngster, Brando was aggressive and rebellious – his spell in a military academy ending in expulsion, after which he took off for New York where he enrolled under Stella Adler in what was later to become the Actors' Studio. There he learned the Stanislavsky 'Method', a naturalistic approach to acting and character interpretation, and became the cinema's first notable exponent of the style (Brando starred in films several years before James Dean). It provided the foundations of his extraordinary technical skills, but was nevertheless the medium of, rather than the source for, his own disturbing presence as the brute male: bulky, crude and unwashed, he represents a primitive and uncompromising eroticism. But Brando is more than a big slob – his power and his threat lie in his frightening seriousness, and the sense of unreleased passion one can only just glimpse.

Brando became a star via Broadway, playing the crass, mumbling, violent Stanley Kowalski who rapes his nymphomaniac sister-in-law in Tennessee Williams's 'A Streetcar Named

RIGHT: studio portrait, 1950.
   Photographer John Engstead

ABOVE: *A Streetcar Named Desire*, 1951, with Vivien Leigh
OPPOSITE: studio portrait, c. 1949

Desire'. Of the film offers which subsequently deluged him, he accepted the role of a paraplegic war veteran in *The Men*, 1950; Brando characteristically moved into a veterans' hospital to prepare for it, even insisting that a urine bottle be strapped to his leg. A year later, he recreated his stage role for the screen version of *Streetcar*, with Vivien Leigh. Even though the script was inevitably toned down by the Hays Office, the movie was magnificent and was hugely successful at the box office, making Brando a major screen star.

He went on to take some of the classic leading-men roles of the fifties. After *Viva Zapata!*, 1952, for which his make-up included the painful insertion of plastic rings into his nostrils to flair them, and Antony in *Julius Caesar*, in 1953, he showed that the power of his presence and technical ability were more effective in contemporary drama: as ex-boxer Terry Malloy, 'I could have been a contender . . . instead of a bum', in the classic *On the Waterfront*, 1954, a Damon Runyon gambler in *Guys and Dolls*, 1955, and the motorbike rebel of *The Wild One* in 1953.

Brando's own love life was always stormy. He had short affairs with Shelley Winters and Eva Marie Saint, among others, and a more complicated one with France Nuyen; they had a son and she had a nervous breakdown. In *Reflections in a Golden*

Eye, 1967, he played an army officer, a repressed homosexual, patting his hair and smiling vainly as he lusts after private Robert Forster. Allegations of homosexuality never bothered him, 'Like a large number of men', he once said, 'I too have had homosexual experiences, and I'm not ashamed'. His first marriage to Anna Kashfi, in 1957, resulted in copious sordid revelations after the relationship fell apart in 1959; his second marriage, to Movita, a Mexican actress he met during the filming of *Viva Zapata!,* was also turbulent. More recently he set up home with a Tahitian girl, Tarita, in isolation

RIGHT: *On the Waterfront*, 1954, with
     Eva Marie Saint
BELOW: *The Wild One*, 1953, with Mary Murphy

on an island, and is fiercely protective of their privacy.

The sixties marked a fall in Brando's popularity. Most of his films either did badly financially, or did him little credit; he also fell out with Hollywood. In 1972, he triumphantly resuscitated his career with a superb piece of character acting in the role of Don Corleone in *The Godfather*, for which he won an Oscar; characteristically, caring little for Hollywood's ways, he asked an unknown American Indian actress to turn down the award on his behalf because of 'the treatment of American Indians in the motion picture industry'. Later, though, he was to give the finest per-

formance of his career in *Last Tango in Paris*, producing all the primitiveness and potency of his youth as he takes Maria Schneider to the depths of sexual humiliation. At the end, when Schneider shoots him, he takes the chewing-gum from his mouth and puts it neatly under some railings before he crumples to the floor, dead – a classic Brando moment.

ABOVE: publicity portrait for *Last Tango in Paris*, 1972

THE SIXTIES

The sixties produced some of the greatest upheavals in Hollywood and European cinema since the advent of sound in the late twenties. Power shifted to the people who actually made the films. The studio system had fallen apart and television had changed the structure of the audience. McCarthy's outcasts from the witch-hunt of the early fifties were rebuilding their careers and some American film-makers, forced by currency restrictions to work abroad, were encountering new and invigorating influences in Europe: the gifted young directors of the *nouvelle vague* like Truffaut and Godard emerged in French cinema and British directors like Karel Reisz and Tony Richardson were continuing to explore the realism of the fifties in order to capture the changed society around them. The paradigm of the British leading man in the early sixties changed dramatically; Laurence Harvey as Joe Lampton, the ruthless working-class hero who used women to get to the top, and Albert Finney, the restless, rebellious factory hand in *Saturday Night and Sunday Morning*, proved that social values were changing very quickly. Pop stars, like the Beatles, moved over to the screen and audiences were fascinated by any opportunity to look inside Swinging London.

The breakdown of the Hollywood studio system gave stars far greater control of their own destinies, but also handed them far more responsibility. Now, instead of being moulded and projected by the studio machinery, they had to shape their own image by choosing the right parts on an individual basis, and, if necessary, by moving into production in order to control the quality and marketing of the finished product. Too many box-office flops and they would be in trouble; but if they took the right decisions they could move into super-stardom. The first moves in that direction had been made in the fifties, but the star as producer and controller – an unheard of phenomenon since Chaplin, Fairbanks and Pickford formed United Artists in the twenties – started to become the norm in the sixties.

The traditional concept of the leading man was also undermined by changing sexual attitudes and the advance of feminism. In the thirties, when the majority of male screen archetypes had been established, the leading man and his lady had been playing to a family audience as a result of the Hays Code. There was strict censorship and no hanky-panky, although of course the restraint itself was tantalizingly sexual and better film-makers became astute at intimation: Tracy drawing the drapes around the four-poster he shares with Hepburn in *Adam's Rib*; William Powell peeling a banana as Virginia Valli undresses in the early *Paid to Love*. Now, with the loosening of censorship a great deal more was allowed. Subjects were covered that Hollywood had previously deemed too depressing for audiences. Leading men could be seen as flawed characters, such as losers and drunks, and even the old stereotypes were not what they seemed. A nude was no longer rude if it moved and sex on the screen became explicit. During the same ten years Hollywood continued to project women on the screen as daffy housewives, sizzling sex bombs and predatory ballbreakers, but this began to look ridiculous given the emergence of the skinny sixties girl, and the tentative dismantling of such stereotypes in the work of younger film directors. Monroe's death in 1962 and the fading popularity of the other outsize sex queen, Jayne Mansfield, who was used to satirize the Monroe type, at the beginning of the sixties, marked the death of a certain kind of leading woman. Women were increasingly being used as subject rather than object; *Far from the Madding Crowd*, for instance, was about Julie Christie, not Alan Bates, Terence Stamp or Peter Finch, the men in her life. Eventually, this could make the leading man irrelevant.

While it was clear that traditional archetypes for the leading man had also to be reconsidered, the studios and producers were not quite sure what they wanted the public to see and they threw out a maelstrom of types. Some actors came out of the old stock of moulds: Rock Hudson survived as the handsome, uncomplicated beefcake, Omar Sharif was the industry's new liquid-eyed exotic and George Segal's witty urbane sophistication was reminiscent of the thirties man-about-town.

But by the end of the decade, the social and political turmoil of the sixties had left its mark. Certain types simply went out of fashion. If the fifties had closed with the demise of the swashbuckler, the cynical sixties showed the door to all-conquering heroic types like Charlton Heston, who at the beginning of the sixties had still been making costume epics and all-star action spectaculars like *El Cid* and *The Greatest Story Ever Told*. That kind of all-powerful mythic hero was replaced by the man of action and the sympathetic outsider: Steve McQueen turned up in *The Magnificent Seven* and, more significantly, *The Great Escape* which was one of the first international casts put together by the studios in an attempt to draw television audiences back to the wide screen. A little later *The Dirty Dozen* developed the theme of the all-male group with its own internal code of loyalty and honour, foreshadowing the buddy movie of the late sixties and early seventies like *Butch Cassidy and the Sundance Kid*. After a false start as a Brando clone in the fifties, Paul Newman gave the action man a light, sophisticated veneer, and Clint

Eastwood emerged from Italian spaghetti Westerns which used harsh, almost stylized, violence, to become a star of the sixties and a superstar of the seventies as the late twentieth-century loner battling against society's bureaucracies in defence of individual values.

The old-fashioned fantasy hero found an up-dated form in the gangster and spy movie. In France, the genre threw up Alain Delon whose off-screen lifestyle reinforced his screen image, and Jean-Paul Belmondo, who was first brought to attention internationally as a 'Bogey'-type character in Godard's film *Breathless*. In Britain, Sean Connery hit exactly the right degree of self-parody as James Bond while Michael Caine created the seedy Harry Palmer of *The Ipcress File*.

Viewing the decade as a whole, there were not only significant changes but also some genuinely new types. The films emanating from England in the early sixties introduced working-class heroes, like Harvey and Finney; Michael Caine swung his way through a bunch of guts and ladies in *Alfie*, while Terence Stamp and David Hemmings personified a slightly different but equally attractive sort of leading man: classless, beautiful and part of the young elite of swinging London. Meanwhile, in Italy, Marcello Mastroianni was making dissipation sexy.

In America new directors like Robert Altman and Mike Nichols boosted the careers of offbeat leading men like Donald Sutherland and Dustin Hoffman who shared a half-tamed, slightly sleazy and disturbing sexuality which caught the mood of the end of the decade. For the first time, too, a leading man could be black although, as Sidney Poitier discovered, it would be nearly impossible to find good roles.

CHARLTON HESTON

Charlton Heston's strapping, rough-hewn physique, sonorous voice and the intense, slightly tragic cast of his expression were part of a hulking screen presence that never got lost among the spectacular scenery, special effects and noisy battles that always seem to surround him. His strongest and sexiest role was as a Mexican drugs cop in Welles's *Touch of Evil*, 1958, with its steamy, exotic atmosphere, but the fans preferred to see him as beefcake in big-budget costume epics. He launched into them with *The Ten Commandments*, 1956, in which he doubled as Moses and the voice of God, won an Oscar for his gigantic portrayal of legendary hero *Ben-Hur*, 1959, and followed it up with an equally dominating performance as *El Cid*, 1961. In *The War Lord*, 1965, he was cast in the romantic hero mould as a medieval knight, but *Khartoum*, 1966, took him back to the desert and gave him the opportunity to explore a more complex character, General Gordon. During the sixties, his kind of mythic hero went out of fashion and he began to tackle different kinds of roles, shedding his heroic persona for the illiterate cowboy who didn't wash too often in *Will Penny*, 1968, taking on Shakespeare in the British *Julius Caesar*, 1970, and behaving nobly in disaster spectaculars like *Earthquake* and *Airport 1975*.

OPPOSITE: studio portrait, 1950.
Photographer Bud Fraker
ABOVE: *Ben-Hur*, 1959
LEFT: *Touch of Evil*, 1958, with Janet Leigh

LAURENCE HARVEY

Haunted-looking and cold-eyed, Laurence Harvey created a classic mid-sixties figure in Schlesinger's film *Darling*, 1965, as the world-weary man who is eager for, yet jaundiced by, sensation. He had first shown his penchant for playing callous and clever charmers as the ambitious Joe Lampton in *Room at the Top*, a key British film of the late fifties which wiped away much of the romantic veneer from sex.

In earlier times, Harvey would probably have been catalogued as an exotic. The son of Jewish Lithuanian parents, he had emigrated to South Africa when he was six, but returned to England to study at RADA. *Room at the Top*, opposite award-winning Simone Signoret, had won him an Oscar nomination, and he followed it with another strong performance as the ambitious promoter in *Expresso Bongo*, 1959. Soon afterwards he went to Hollywood to make *The Alamo*, and be a married man pursued by Elizabeth Taylor in *Butterfield 8*, 1960; however, his British films, like *Life at the Top* and *Darling*, for which his co-star Julie Christie won an Oscar, gave him better roles. Off screen, he had several relationships with older women, including Hermione Baddeley, Margaret Leighton and Joan Cohn, the last two of whom he married. His final marriage was to model Paulene Stone, a year before his death from cancer in 1973.

ABOVE: *Room at the Top*, 1958, with Simone Signoret

172

DIRK BOGARDE

In the sixties, Dirk Bogarde left behind his fifties matinée idol roles to emerge as a serious actor of international distinction, particularly in his work for director Joseph Losey. He brought a superbly chilling nastiness to Losey's *The Servant*, 1963, in the part of the manipulative manservant who gradually destroys his foppish young employer, and followed it with fine performances in *King and Country*, *Darling* and *Modesty Blaise*.

Of Dutch descent, but born in London, Bogarde made his name in *The Blue Lamp*, 1949, as the rude young boy who kills a sympathetic older policeman in a shoot-out. For the time, it was heady stuff, but he was subsequently groomed by the Rank studios as a British matinée idol, an image best remembered in the part of fun-loving medic Simon Sparrow in *Doctor in the House*, 1954, and its sequels. Now openly bi-sexual, he was the first big star to tackle a portrayal of a homosexual leading man, in *Victim*, 1961, and ten years later was brilliant in Visconti's *Death in Venice*, playing the composer obsessed with a beautiful boy in a Venice ravaged by cholera.

Fassbinder's *Despair*, 1978, placed him as a Russian émigré in Germany, facing both marital and financial failure. He now lives in France, writing as well as acting; his autobiographies, 'A Postilion Struck by Lightning' and 'Snakes and Ladders', met with critical acclaim and he has recently published his first novel.

ABOVE: publicity portrait for *The Singer Not the Song*, 1960

173

ALBERT FINNEY

A leading actor rather than a leading man, Albert Finney's first starring role, opposite Rachel Roberts and Shirley Ann Field in the classic *Saturday Night and Sunday Morning*, 1960, immediately launched him as a British romantic hero. It was sexy to be working-class; his angry factory worker, Arthur Seaton – a young man imprisoned as much by his own desires as by the poverty of his background, but rebellious and proud – is one of the most enduring screen personas of British film in the sixties.

Finney was born in Lancashire and graduated from RADA to work on the West End stage. He followed his initial success with a Rabelaisian performance in *Tom Jones* in 1963 as the cheerfully randy young hero of Fielding's picaresque novel. Rich enough to pick and choose his films after that, he made the smart comedy of marriage manners *Two for the Road*, 1966, with Audrey Hepburn and the next year directed himself in the hugely underrated *Charlie Bubbles*, a melancholy piece about a successful writer adrift from his working class roots, with ex-wife Billie Whitelaw and secretary/

lover Liza Minnelli. In *Gumshoe*, 1971, he was a marvellously seedy bingo-caller whose Marlowe-style private-eye fantasies become grim reality. Married to, and now divorced from, the French actress Anouk Aimée, Finney's main interest is now the stage, although he continues to find interesting leading-actor roles in such films as *Shoot the Moon*, *The Dresser* and *Under the Volcano*.

ABOVE: publicity portrait for *Tom Jones*, 1963

DAVID HEMMINGS

Small and slightly built he had the looks of a raddled choirboy — he made his show business debut at the age of nine when, as a boy soprano, he toured with the English Opera Group. David Hemmings became the archetypal face of the sixties in *Blow-Up*, 1966, Antonioni's marvellously chilling portrait of Swinging London. Hemmings plays Thomas, the photographer who has possibly captured a murder on film and pursues his obsession with it through a quintessentially sixties urban landscape. Since then his career has been less successful, suffering from close identification with his sixties image; he climbed into Victorian military costume for *The Charge of the Light Brigade*, 1968, and sci-fi fancy dress with Jane Fonda in *Barbarella*, the same year. In the seventies he developed an older playboy image, directing rock star David Bowie, and acting himself, in *Just a Gigolo*, 1978. He was married to Gayle Hunnicutt.

ABOVE: *Blow-Up*, 1966, with Vanessa Redgrave
RIGHT: portrait, 1966

TERENCE STAMP

Terence Stamp started his film career representing the innocence of sixties Youth. His thuggish prettiness, hypnotic blue eyes and off-hand manner were perfectly suited to roles as comely yobs and cads elevated to romantic status by love. But unlike some of his contemporaries, he managed to mature and play men of experience, and his best work suggested a working-class Paul Newman.

Picked out of stage rep to play the lead in Peter Ustinov's 1962 movie *Billy Budd* (about the destruction of an innocent) when he was only twenty-two, Stamp was also cast that year as the young lout in *Term of Trial*. Afraid of being type-cast, he delayed his next appearance for three years, resurfacing in a completely different mood in *The Collector* as the creepy bank clerk who collects butterflies and kidnaps art student Samantha Eggar and holds her prisoner. His next two roles were equally unpredictable: in 1966 he appeared in the comic strip-inspired thriller *Modesty Blaise* and in 1966 he was the chillingly caddish sergeant loved by Julie Christie in *Far from the Madding Crowd*.

In the same year, he was a romantic hero of sorts in the working-class documentary drama *Poor Cow*, playing Carol White's lover amongst the squalor. He won acclaim for his performance in *The Mind of Mr Soames*, 1969, then disappeared for much of the seventies to reappear in *Superman*, 1978, as an inhabitant of Krypton alongside Marlon Brando and Susannah York.

LEFT: *Poor Cow*, 1967, with Carol White
OPPOSITE: publicity portrait for *Billy Budd*, 1962

ALAN BATES

Alan Bates's persona began, rather like that of Albert Finney, in the working-class mould: in *A Kind of Loving*, 1962, he played an aspiring, thoughtful young man who gets his girlfriend, June Ritchie, pregnant and does the honourable thing although he no longer loves her. Although remaining very British, his image developed quite differently from Finney's: as that of the ideal lover, chunkily handsome, efficient in bed, but with qualities to attract the thinking woman. He was loyal to Julie Christie as the sturdy yeoman lover of *Far from the Madding Crowd*, and sensitive as Ursula's lover in Ken Russell's *Women in Love* (known for the fireside nude wrestling scene with Oliver Reed).

He first achieved international acclaim in *Zorba the Greek*, 1964, and was nominated for the best-actor Oscar for his performance as a wrongly imprisoned Russian Jewish peasant in *The Fixer*, 1968, but it was his role of the successful, manly painter who becomes Jill Clayburgh's lover in *An Unmarried Woman* in 1978 that brought him major Hollywood stardom.

Having learnt his craft at London's innovative Royal Court Theatre he still performs regularly on stage as well as in television drama and on screen.

LEFT: publicity portrait for *Far from the Madding Crowd*, 1967

PETER O'TOOLE

Rakishly handsome, with intensely blue eyes glittering behind his desert gear, Peter O'Toole became the thinking woman's romantic hero as the confused and complex adventurer, T. E. Lawrence, in David Lean's epic *Lawrence of Arabia*, 1962. Since then, his career has had a rather hit-and-miss quality.

Although he later showed a roguish touch in comedy, playing the twitchy ladies' man in *What's New Pussycat?*, 1965, he seemed to prefer portraying introverted loners, obsessives or even mystics. In *Lord Jim*, 1965, he was disastrous as an idealist who redeemed himself after an act of cowardice; in *Man of La Mancha*, 1972, he was the deluded Don Quixote; and in *The Ruling Class*, 1972, he played the mad young aristocrat who thinks he is God. He also played Henry II twice, first opposite Richard Burton in *Becket*, 1964, and then in *The Lion in Winter*, 1968, opposite Katharine Hepburn.

O'Toole was born in Connemara, Ireland, but brought up in England; he received his stage education at RADA, and later at the Bristol Old Vic. O'Toole always retained a strong affection for the theatre and during the seventies and eighties he has taken on an increasing amount of stage work, often with controversial results. In 1982, he made his nicest film, *My Favourite Year*, playing a drunk, aging matinée idol — some say Barrymore, some say Flynn — who is attempting to make a comeback via fifties television.

RIGHT: publicity portrait for *Lawrence of Arabia*, 1962

SEAN CONNERY

The James Bond spy thrillers made Sean Connery one of the biggest screen sex symbols in the world. Accessorized by small guns and a bevy of glamorous ladies, he lent Ian Fleming's smoothie spy the necessary wit and protective virility to make him hugely appealing as a fantasy lover and hero for the sixties. Debonair in a rugged Scottish way, he was extraordinarily sexy, upper class but cosmopolitan and able to take on all comers.

The first Bond movie, the enormously successful *Dr No*, 1962, was followed by *From Russia with Love*, 1963, *Goldfinger*, 1964, and *Thunderball*, 1965. Connery was already trying to break away from the image, as the forceful Mark Rutland in *Marnie*, 1964, and as the obsessively rebellious prisoner in *The Hill*, 1965. However, he has found it difficult to leave Bond behind and exploit his quality of glossy butchiness in more intelligent films, in part because his fans have not wanted him to: neither Roger Moore nor George Lazenby have lived up to his success in the role. He made two more Bond movies, *You Only Live Twice*, 1967, and *Diamonds Are Forever*, 1971, then took on a variety of new roles, notably *The Anderson Tapes*, 1971, and *The Man Who Would Be King*, 1975. But the suave spy continued to dog him – he returned to the screen as Bond in *Never Say Never Again*, a reworking of *Thunderball*, made outside the control of Bond movie creator and producer 'Cubby' Broccoli.

LEFT: *From Russia with Love*, 1963

MICHAEL CAINE

Michael Caine is an odd mixture of working-class charm and aristocratic arrogance, qualities which belie the ordinariness of his looks and which were at their most potent in *Alfie*, 1966, in which he chatted numerous females into bed and trouble without a hint of chivalry or remorse. The appeal of his mild-mannered toughness had been made clear by *The Ipcress File*, 1965, as the seedily heroic, bespectacled spy Harry Palmer, a leading man almost despite himself; a complete contrast to those two glossy British heroes, Sean Connery and Roger Moore, but it had taken the sexier image to make the appeal stick.

Born Maurice Micklewhite, in London, Caine had worked in the repertory theatre and for television and — rather ironically, given his later image — had his first big success as an aristocratic officer in *Zulu*, 1964. In the late sixties he went on to make several war films and thrillers, the best of which were *Gambit*, 1966, opposite Shirley MacLaine, and *The Italian Job*, 1969, a lovely caper/crime movie in which Caine played a small-time spiv running a big continental bullion robbery.

Caine underwent a re-evaluation in the seventies taking more serious roles in such films as *Sleuth*, 1972, and *The Man Who Would Be King* and in *The Romantic Englishwoman*, both 1975, in the latter playing a writer of fantasy fiction married to the discontented Glenda Jackson. Now in his fifties, he has retained his aura of appealing self-mockery, and in 1983 he was wonderful as the oddly romantic, academic drunk who falls for Julie Walters in *Educating Rita*.

RIGHT: publicity portrait for *Deadfall*, 1968

STEVE McQUEEN

A toughie with an affinity for hardware – guns, motorbikes, sports cars and handcuffs – Steve McQueen's leading men were stoical, cool and insolent loners, like the hero of *Bullitt*, the movie with the car chase to end all car chases, in which his persistent cop wins through as a human extension of a big, powerful, pulsating engine. Much seems to have been based on McQueen's own off-screen taste for racing cars and bikes.

Brought up by his grandparents, he was a troublesome adolescent who spent three years in a California reformatory, ran away from home and became a drifter, working on ships, as an oil-field labourer and as a fairground barker. Of his three-year stint with the navy he spent forty-one days in detention, suggesting that it was just as well he discovered he could act and found a place at drama school. He once said of himself, 'There's something about my shaggy-dog eyes that makes people think I'm good, but I'm really not all that good. I'm pretty much myself most of the time in my movies, and I've accepted that'. Like James Coburn, McQueen first shone in *The Magnificent Seven*, 1960, then went on to play the taciturn loner in *Hell is for Heroes*, 1962, and the heroic motorcycle freak of *The Great Escape*, 1963, who is captured bloodily entangled with his machinery in the barbed wire, and returned to the P.O.W. camp 'cooler'.

His heroes were often made unconventional by sensitivity and self-doubt, characteristics which extended his appeal to women as well as men. Of his roles in the sixties, the most interesting were the professional gambler in *The Cincinnati Kid*, 1965, the half-Indian cowboy tracking down his parents' killers in *Nevada Smith*, 1966, and as the ship's engineer attracted to Candice Bergen in *The Sand Pebbles*, 1966. In 1968 he abandoned his macho image for that of a more traditional romantic leading man in *The Thomas Crown Affair*, opposite Faye

LEFT: *The Great Escape*, 1963

182

Dunaway, in which he took the part of a seemingly respectable businessman who turns out to be in the business of robbing banks. It was his silliest movie, but by then he was a superstar.

In *Junior Bonner*, 1972, he reverted to his established persona to play an aging rodeo star and the same year, in *The Getaway*, he got mixed up with bank robbery, and with Ali MacGraw, who later became his second wife. *Papillon*, 1973, produced another characteristically tough, resilient performance as the real-life convict who battles to escape from cruelty and squalor on Devil's Island. He completed his last film, *Tom Horn*, 1980, while undergoing treatment for cancer; his third wife, Barbara Minty, was with him when he died the same year, following surgery, aged fifty.

RIGHT: publicity portrait for *Bullitt*, 1968
BELOW: *Love with the Proper Stranger*, 1963, with Natalie Wood

Born in Florida of West Indian parents, Poitier was the first black American to become a leading man. He obligingly became the standard-bearer of racial harmony in *In the Heat of the Night*, 1967, as Virgil Tibbs, the young homicide officer working under a racist police chief played by Rod Steiger. In the same year he also starred in *To Sir with Love* and played the unthreateningly polite, handsome and successful fiancé of Katharine Houghton in *Guess Who's Coming to Dinner*, the first film to confront, if not completely successfully, the black/white sex barrier. Subsequently he tended to be cast as a nice, safe, well-educated black, and so turned to producing and directing, as well as acting, in the seventies, notably with Bill Cosby. But eventually he chose to retire, commenting that he no longer wished to act because film parts for blacks were only ever as mindless bullies, braggarts, sex-machines and song-and-dance men.

RIGHT: publicity portrait for *Guess Who's Coming to Dinner*, 1967

OPPOSITE: *The Thomas Crown Affair*, 1968, with Faye Dunaway

ALAIN DELON

Alain Delon's romantic gangster image has been augmented by his underworld associations, particularly since they received a public airing after his bodyguard was murdered in 1968. Delon was cleared of any involvement in the scandal that followed, and the incident only served to bolster his screen persona: the following year he had a huge success in the blood-stained *Borsalino*, which he also produced, playing a small-time gangster who, with Jean-Paul Belmondo, becomes king of the Marseilles thirties underworld. Discovered at the 1957 Cannes Film Festival, he initially turned down a Hollywood contract to work with European directors, becoming a star as the young American who envies Maurice Ronet's possessions and girl and sets out to impersonate him in *Plein Soleil*, a 1960 thriller, and giving good performances for Visconti in *Rocco and His Brothers*, 1960, and *The Leopard*, 1963. During the mid-sixties, he enjoyed a brief but not terribly successful international career, notably as an Italian gigolo opposite Shirley MacLaine in *The Yellow Rolls-Royce*, 1964.

It was only in the late sixties that the sleek and lethal Delon came to epitomize the calm, psychopathic hoodlum, staring into the camera like a cat assessing a mouse. His tough, ruthless side was first used to real effect by Jean-Pierre Melville in *Le Samourai*, 1967, which was followed by *Le Cercle Rouge*, 1970, and *Dirty Money*, 1972. The success of *Borsalino* brought further lucrative ventures into production, so much so that in 1985, he moved to Switzerland, claiming that he found it intolerable to live under the French socialist government.

LEFT: portrait, c. 1968

JEAN-PAUL BELMONDO

Belmondo rose to overnight fame as the Bogart-worshipping anti-hero of *Breathless*, 1960, and, with a notable performance as the slightly deranged hero of *Pierrot Le Fou*, 1965, established himself as an existentialist figurehead to the rebellious youth of the sixties with a persona that contained elements of James Dean, Humphrey Bogart, and even Marlon Brando.

Simultaneously abrasive, sensitive, anti-social and tender, his outlaw image is less chillingly psychopathic than that of Alain Delon, with whom he revelled in new excesses of criminality in *Borsalino*, 1970; his dog-eared features and hurt, resigned eyes contrast engagingly with Delon's icy prettiness. The son of a sculptor, he went on to take over from Jean Gabin as France's most popular screen star, an actor of great virtuosity who has played roles ranging from louts to students to factory workers, priests and even a French Robin Hood in *Cartouche*, 1962. Nowadays he tends to stick to playing his gangster persona in commercial, lighthearted thrillers, and his notable appearances in the seventies included the swindling protagonist of *Stavisky*, 1974, in which he invested money; he now heads his own production company.

RIGHT: publicity portrait for *Moderato Cantabile*, 1960

MARCELLO MASTROIANNI

International popularity came Mastroianni's way through the Fellini film *La Dolce Vita* in 1960, when his lovely eyes and gloomy intimacy made his character – a journalist caught up in the decadent *malaise* of modern Rome – sympathetic despite its emptiness. Later film critic Alexander Walker said of him, 'What makes up for his deficiency is the wishful thinking of his mass public, in the main female and romantic, which is attracted by the sight of him as a suitable case for their care and at the same time aroused by the thought of him with all his powers restored'.

Born near Rome, and originally an office clerk, Mastroianni had worked in the theatre and was already a success-ful star in the Italian cinema before *La Dolce Vita*. As his screen career progressed in the sixties, he developed a constantly world-weary, sated persona and his performances were divided rather unhappily between generally interesting ones in Italian films and ineffectual ones in international productions, playing modern Latin lovers with beautiful women flocking around him. Thus he turned in good performances in Antonioni's *La Notte*, 1961, as a bored novelist married to Jeanne Moreau, and in Fellini's *8½*, 1963, as a creatively impotent film director. But he disappointed in *Divorce Italian Style*, 1961, in which he played a Sicilian count trying to get his dreary wife to compromise herself so that he could marry his pretty cousin, and *Marriage Italian Style*, 1964, in which he played a flashy playboy behaving like a cad to Sophia Loren. In the seventies, he was particularly good as the rich, weary aristocrat in John Boorman's *Leo the Last*, 1970, and gave one of his finest, and most grotesque, performances in *La Grande Bouffe*, which is also known as *Blow-Out*, in 1973.

ABOVE: *8½*, 1963

Once compared by TV critic Clive James to 'a box of dates smouldering with passion', Omar Sharif was already Egypt's top male star when David Lean cast him as Peter O'Toole's sheikh chum in *Lawrence of Arabia*, 1962, then as Julie Christie's faithful Russian doctor in *Dr Zhivago*, 1965, the two films which earned him international heart-throb status. They also provided him with his most famous and archetypal roles, as an exotic with a noble profile and a romantic, idealistic spirit.

Sharif also simmered in several less demanding roles as a latter-day Latin lover with a heroic streak: a Yugoslav partisan in love with Ingrid Bergman in *The Yellow Rolls-Royce*, 1964, an Austrian crown prince in *Mayerling*, 1968, and a Russian military attaché in love with Julie Andrews in *The Tamarind Seed*, 1974. In *Funny Girl*, 1968, he had a change of pace as the no-good gambler married to Fanny Brice (Barbra Streisand) and in *The Appointment*, 1969, he was a rather wooden contemporary lover businessman enjoying an affair in glamorous Rome with Anouk Aimée. Possibly because of the dullness of all these roles, he now prefers to indulge his passion for playing bridge.

RIGHT: publicity portrait for *Lawrence of Arabia*, 1962

189

WARREN BEATTY

Beatty's superstar persona is that of a charismatic, but ultimately helpless, male moved by forces beyond his control; it is that combination of rebellion and impotence, as well as his traditional good looks, which makes him so attractive. The image was first defined in *Bonnie and Clyde*, 1967, in which he played the wayward and impotent small-time crook, Clyde Barrow, whose semi-comic exploits with Faye Dunaway ended in bloody retribution from the establishment. In fact, having been impressed by the script, Beatty had hired the director, Arthur Penn, produced the film himself and forced the studio to redistribute it after initial box-office failure — an indication of his considerable entrepreneurial abilities which were to emerge more clearly over the next decade.

The younger brother of Shirley MacLaine, Beatty made his debut in Kazan's *Splendor in the Grass*, 1961, and found one of his most interesting early starring roles as the neurotic nightclub comic in *Mickey One*, his first film with Arthur Penn. After the success of *Bonnie and Clyde*, he co-scripted and produced *Shampoo*, 1975, playing the Beverly Hills super-stud hairdresser who beds his steady (Goldie Hawn) and his rival's wife, daughter and mistress (Julie Christie) in the course of the working day. The leading-man image suggested by the movie was enhanced by the fact he had yet to be pinned down in his private life.

Since then Beatty has produced, co-scripted and starred in two more major films. In the first, *Heaven Can Wait*, 1978, he played an American footballer who dies before schedule, and is sent back to earth to occupy the body of a tycoon in order to undo the character's anti-social business practices. The second, *Reds*, 1981, a big-screen political epic, traced the career of John Reed, a founder of the American Communist party, and featured a great on- and off-screen romance with Diane Keaton.

OPPOSITE: *All Fall Down*, 1962
ABOVE: *Bonnie and Clyde*, 1967, with Faye Dunaway

GEORGE SEGAL

Segal was born in New York and his persona, whether in comedies, serious drama or spy thrillers, is very much that of the modern city-dweller: cynical, sophisticated and hard-working, usually middle-class and quite conventional, but attractively defence-less in his emotional life. In the sixties he took on roles as varied as the young professor in *Who's Afraid of Virginia Woolf?* and the down-at-heel spy in *The Quiller Memorandum*, both 1966. Subsequently, he has become rather more suave, showing his affinity for roles which use his humour to explore the pressures on urban man. He showed himself man enough to go for more than just a pretty face in *A Touch of Class*, 1973, in which he plays a happily married man in love with a prickly fashion designer, Glenda Jackson, and *The Owl and the Pussycat*, 1970, in which he was paired with another *jolie-laide*, Barbra Streisand as a kookie hooker. In *Loving*, 1970, he played a commercial artist trapped in the wife-or-mistress dilemma again and, three years later, he made *Blume In Love*, in which the persona has become an ex-married man with the dilemma still unresolved as Segal contemplates an affair with his former wife, Susan Anspach. Robert Altman's *California Split*, 1974, teamed him effectively with Elliott Gould as a man with gambling fever and the more louche side of his persona was also seen in *The Duchess and the Dirtwater Fox*, 1976, in which he was a slightly incompetent rogue partnered by a hooker again.

LEFT: portrait, c. 1970

goods industry was not for him, he handed over to his brother and, after drama school, ended up in New York at Lee Strasberg's Actors' Studio.

His first screen roles were very much in the Brando mould – neurotic, mirthless, mumbling and bolshy. Like him, he played Tennessee Williams's anti-heroes, in *Cat on a Hot Tin Roof*, 1958, and *Sweet Bird of Youth*, 1962, for which he received the first of his Oscar nominations; at one stage he was even labelled the New Brando. Within a few years, though, a new and more distinctive character was emerging – a male whose macho demeanour and tongue-in-cheek bravado concealed sexual fears and social inadequacy. In *The Hustler*, 1961, *Hud*, 1963, and *Cool Hand Luke*, 1967, he displayed a mixture of strength, devilment and vulnerability with which many men could identify. These 'loner' films gave way to the individualist heroes of the early to mid-seventies, notably in *The Life and Times of Judge Roy Bean*, 1972, and *Buffalo Bill and the Indians*, 1976. Newman's sexual attractiveness continued into middle-age despite, or perhaps because of, his honesty in playing characters vulnerable to the disillusioning and depleting forces of time. One of his outstanding performances of the seventies was in *Slap Shot*, 1977, playing a battered, foul-mouthed coach of a washed-up ice hockey team. Far from gliding into distinguished seniority as an aging sex-symbol, Newman also relished the opportunity to present himself as unglamorously as possible as an alcoholic failed lawyer in *The Verdict*, 1981.

In certain ways, Newman's private life conforms to the image of a Hollywood star; one of his great interests is racing cars, which he drives to a very high standard with several wins to his credit. But in other ways he remains an outsider. He is embarrassed by all the

OPPOSITE: *Somebody Up There Likes Me*, 1956
ABOVE: *From the Terrace*, 1960, with
    Joanne Woodward
LEFT: *Cat on a Hot Tin Roof*, 1958, with
    Elizabeth Taylor

ABOVE: *Butch Cassidy and the Sundance Kid*, 1969, with Robert Redford
OPPOSITE: publicity portrait for *The Sting*, 1973

adulation that still comes his way, and is said to regard being asked to remove his dark glasses in the same way most women feel about being asked to expose their breasts. A vociferous liberal who actively participated in the Civil Rights movement and campaigns for the Democrats and gay rights, he often expresses boredom with acting. Newman has two daughters from his first marriage to Jacqueline Witter — their son Scott, a drama student, died in 1978 of a drug and alcohol overdose — and three daughters from his second marriage. He has acted with, or directed, wife Joanne Woodward in a string of films, from *Rachel Rachel*, 1968, and *Winning*, 1969, to *Harry and Son*, 1984, which have always been interesting and sometimes very good.

MODERN TIMES

Our view of modern times is still too obscured by the nearness to the subject to achieve a sharp perspective – although perhaps the lack of focus tends to give a more truthful view. Nevertheless, the eighties do have a distinct and decidedly different character from that of the seventies.

Commercial constraints have had a powerful effect on output. The expansion of the Australian film industry after the government made finance available in the early seventies has produced outstanding films; Mel Gibson has already emerged as an international star from it. Hollywood, meanwhile, is trying to find a solution in the 'blockbuster' approach, making a smaller number of expensive movies guaranteed to do well at the box-office rather than the wide range of middle-budget, something-for-everyone features that pro-liferated in the early seventies. The British film industry has been stimulated by Channel Four, the new inde-pendent television channel, to encourage development of low-budget productions, but is increasingly frus-trated by lack of government support.

By the end of the sixties, the studios decided there was life after television, if only they could make the films people wanted to see. They regrouped and started, therefore, to create stars again. Superstars like Clint Eastwood, Robert Redford, Burt Reynolds and the hardwearing Paul Newman brought in millions of dollars in profit. In Eastwood, the audience saw America's ideal male – tough but sometimes tender, wise but occasionally reckless, and sexy without being obvious about it. Redford personified the honourable, anti-urban hero, although often examining the successful, ruthless and rich in his roles. Reynolds was the virile comedian. Newman just went on thumbing his nose at people in

his own inimitable way. And in the period when the pop music industry was going through a low, youth once again turned to a movie star for its hero – John Travolta, who, briefly, was as famous as Valentino.

At the same time, a new breed of director was emerging: the 'movie brats' like Steven Spielberg and George Lucas; British directors like Ridley Scott and Alan Parker who transferred from commercials. Often, like Martin Scorsese, they were the product of the university film schools, and, as a result, brought a more intellectual approach to movie making. The audience structure was changing once more. The new steady moviegoers were turning out to be under thirty, with, or on the way to, a university degree. Their leading men were Dustin Hoffman, Jack Nicholson and Woody Allen. These were males who did not correspond to traditional ideas of screen masculinity. Perceptions of the attractive male had changed a lot. They were confused or anarchic or suffered from urban angst. Some of them were sexy, but by no means desperately good-looking. Woody Allen, bespectacled and twitchy, would have been laughed out of Hollywood in the thirties; in the past the 'intellectual' male tended to be acceptable only if he looked like Cary Grant in *Bringing Up Baby*. Yet here was Allen with some of the in-dustry's most glamorous leading ladies; both on and off screen in the old style.

The seventies was the decade of the police thriller and its spin-off, the vigilante movie. Eastwood's *Dirty Harry* and its sequels reflected the new obsession with law and order, and the dilemma of man in the urban jungle; one of his recent films, *Tightrope*, is about a sado-masochistic cop. Leading men clambered into their uniforms. Donald Sutherland made *Klute*, Al

Pacino was in *Serpico*, Robert De Niro exploded with frustration and violence in *Taxi Driver*. The last three of these foreshadowed the new leading man who struts his stuff rather than reaches into the emotions.

Other trends can also be detected. The plight of man in the nuclear age has been explored; the political events of the sixties, notably Vietnam, have sufficiently receded to become Hollywood subject matter; and the future – space and all that gadgetry – has become good territory for adventure heroes. Harrison Ford is the twenty-first century version of our old friend, the swashbuckler. In the third decade of feminism, the changing definition of the masculine role has resulted in Hoffman movies like *Kramer vs Kramer* and *Tootsie*, and romantic films like *Body Heat* with William Hurt, and *Betrayal*, with Jeremy Irons, which feature men who are dispensed with by their leading ladies. In *An Unmarried Woman*, Jill Clayburgh decides to remain on her own rather than take her husband back or commit herself permanently to her lover, Alan Bates. The violence and frustration of the seventies has given way to a mood of acceptance, ordinariness and conservatism, and there has been a spate of nostalgic films.

Outside influences have shaped the persona as well as the physique of the screen male. The large range of archetypes that existed in the thirties and forties has become irrelevant and inappropriate and masculine power is in the process of redefinition, as shown by the work of actor/director Sam Shepard. The Western obsession with health and fitness has concentrated attention on the body. Superman's torso says it all; the accent on the shoulders, the well-muscled legs. The admired male shape is that of the athlete. Sport, with its stress on the supposedly 'male' qualities of competitiveness, aggression, ruthlessness and physical power, has brought about a new look. In the past, it was women who were treated as cheesecake – now the men are presented in almost the same way.

This could be a reaction to the hormonal confusion of current youth culture, which has reached its apotheosis in the gender-hopping of Boy George and his clones. The cinema has often attempted to resolve its uncertainties by looking back to the more serene days – in this case, the time when men were men and not on-screen bundles of neuroses.

Whatever the reason, the subtlety, sensitivity and intelligence of the seventies male is less visible. Though the shy grace of Sam Shepard recalls Gary Cooper, screen heroes of the eighties are uncomplicated, handsome and virile: they are tall, brooding hulks like Richard Gere and Matt Dillon who carry an overt sexual threat. Ultimately, there is an assumption that however strongly feminism is now part of our culture, a large number of women have sexual reflexes which have hardly changed. Hubby may be washing up in the kitchen and she may be emptying her briefcase after a hard day at the office, but what she secretly longs for is still a dreamboat knocking at the door.

CLINT EASTWOOD

A quiet, self-reliant pussycat, tough with men but tender with chosen women, Clint Eastwood has a lazy, low-profile sexiness and a tantalizingly disciplined tension. Occasionally it metamorphoses into orgiastic viciousness. Although Eastwood is not as rugged as John Wayne, and his persona is neither straightforwardly paternalistic nor law-abiding, he nonetheless became one of America's ideal macho males in the seventies, and he is now usually regarded as the natural successor to Wayne's position as the foremost action film hero. At times, however, as in *Dirty Harry*, when Eastwood tortures a confession out of the killer he has hunted down, the persona is far more anti-heroic.

Much of that solitary persona ties in with Eastwood's own experience; born in San Francisco during the Depression years, he had an itinerant family life while his father travelled to find work. He was a self-sufficient, rather withdrawn boy whose only success at school was athletic. Later, he odd-jobbed as a truck driver and a lumberjack and coached swimming in the army. He drifted into movies through bit-parts and got his break in the television series *Rawhide*, in which he played the boyish, laid-back cowboy Rowdy Yates for seven years.

He first developed the figure of the cynical, idealistic wanderer dishing out revenge in a meaningless universe, as the 'Man with No Name' in Sergio Leone's trilogy of spaghetti Westerns, *A Fistful of Dollars*, 1964, *For a Few Dollars More*, 1965, and *The Good, the Bad and the Ugly*, 1966. The character was quite new – Eastwood recalls that he made it 'much more economical and much less expository' than the way it had originally been written – and was rapturously received. He then transferred the moral law-breaker to a modern, urban context as the cop who

OPPOSITE: *Dirty Harry*, 1971
ABOVE: *Play Misty for Me*, 1971, with Jessica Walter
LEFT: *Every Which Way But Loose*, 1978, with Sondra Locke

201

is not always prepared to go through the bureaucratic channels. In *Coogan's Bluff*, 1968, he played a deputy sheriff from Arizona who goes to New York to bring back a killer, and in *Dirty Harry*, 1971, a cop battling against red tape as he tracks down a sadistic murderer in San Francisco. Explaining the subtlety of his character's relationship with the law, Eastwood once said, 'There is a fantasy figure in this era of bureaucracy, of complicated life, income tax and politicizing everything, that there's a guy who can do certain things by himself. There'll always be that fantasy. I think there's an admiration for it'.

The same year, Eastwood directed and starred in the much under-rated *Play Misty for Me*, taking the role of a disc-jockey unwillingly involved with a homicidal girl fan. Still a loner, the character presented himself more overtly as an emotional/sexual being, aware of a conflict between isolation and intimacy. Again, aspects of the character seemed close to Eastwood himself, a loner who avoids intrusion into his private life. This is also true of his relationships with women; he professes to be deeply in favour of monogamy, and his own marriage, to Maggie Johnson, lasted twenty-eight years.

One of the few superstars around, Eastwood has persevered with directing, accruing most critical acclaim for the epic Western *The Outlaw Josey Wales*, 1976. Eastwood abandoned serious drama to make the comic box-office hit *Every Which Way But Loose*, 1978, starring alongside a gorilla and his real-life companion Sondra Locke, but in *Tightrope* he returned to a darker version of Dirty Harry, as a cop, Wes Block, tracking down a sex killer while himself subject to the same contorted, violent urges that drive his prey.

ABOVE: publicity portrait for *For a Few Dollars More*, 1965

KRIS KRISTOFFERSON

Kristofferson brings to his romantic screen image the laid-back charisma of an ex-rock star and the quiet charm of a brainy Ivy League all-rounder with a mind as well as muscle. He was a Rhodes Scholar at Oxford before doing five years in the army in Germany, then dropped out to Nashville, where he eventually achieved international success as a singer-songwriter; his songs including the classic 'Me and Bobby McGee' for Janis Joplin. Fittingly, his screen image is usually that of the macho attractive anti-hero: a singer in his first major film, *Cisco Pike*, 1971, a romantic outlaw in *Pat Garrett and Billy the Kid*, 1973, a trucker in *Convoy*, 1978, and chosen by Barbra Streisand as the pop star in *A Star is Born*, 1976.

Kristofferson's film career really took off in 1973 in Peckinpah's *Pat Garrett and Billy the Kid*, playing Billy opposite James Coburn, Bob Dylan and Rita Coolidge, whom he married soon afterwards. His quiet, hairy charm then won Ellen Burstyn's heart in Scorsese's *Alice Doesn't Live Here Anymore*, 1975, and he played the sensitive star footballer who shares Jill Clayburgh with Burt Reynolds in *Semi-Tough*, 1977. During the seventies, Kristofferson's private life was less than saintly: he drank a lot until he saw the playback of his alcohol-ridden pop-star character's suicide in *A Star is Born* and immediately identified with it. Divorced, smooth-cheeked and sober, he recently starred in Michael Cimino's *Heaven's Gate*.

RIGHT: studio portrait, 1976

203

BURT REYNOLDS

Energetic and hairy-chested, Burt Reynolds's confidence in his own sexual identity shines through his screen roles whether he is playing as a cop, a footballer or a lovable miscreant. Slightly self-mocking about his footballer physique and private reputation as a virile playboy bachelor, he was the first completely nude male centrefold in 'Cosmopolitan' in 1972 – though it's a decision he has said he regrets.

Born in Georgia, the grandson of a Cherokee Indian, Reynolds was heading for a pro-football career until it was terminated by a car accident. He became a middling star in the late sixties – when he was already moulting at quite a rate – via Westerns, then a major one in John Boorman's *Deliverance*, 1972. In the same year, he dressed up as a nun in *Fuzz*, showing a nice sense of the sexually ridiculous and a flair for hard-edged comedy which has remained his mainstay ever since. *White Lightning*, 1973, introduced the character of Gator, who has appeared in various sequels; in *The Longest Yard*, 1974, he played a convict coaching his fellow inmates for a crunch match against the screws. He played a footballer again in *Semi-Tough*, 1977, stealing Jill Clayburgh from Kris Kristofferson at the end of various louche adventures, and in *Sharky's Machine*, 1981, a demoted cop with an appealing lack of seriousness about busting a crime syndicate with the help of a call-girl ring. Recently, he went through the male menopause in *Starting Over*, and starred in *City Heat*, a romp set in the Prohibition years, with Clint Eastwood.

LEFT: *Sam Whiskey*, 1969

JACK NICHOLSON

JON VOIGHT

Half-tamed and angrily smiling at some private joke, Nicholson is menacingly sexy. The joke – and the threat too – is the knowledge that since life is pointless, you might as well enjoy it on the way. His career has echoed that, moving unconventionally from 'B' movies in the sixties to scriptwriting and then, after his portrayal of the stoned lawyer in *Easy Rider*, 1969, taking off into superstardom. His sleazy, laconic manner makes him well suited to *film noir* and he was outstanding as the sleek but not quite *au fait* investigator in Polanski's *Chinatown*. But his greatest achievement must be the creation of MacMurphy, the martyred agitator of *One Flew Over the Cuckoo's Nest*, whose underlying sanity he made recognizable to an audience of millions.

BELOW: publicity portrait for *Chinatown*, 1974

Voight seems to specialize in leading men duped by the American dream, the innocence of his own boyish looks beautifully conterpointing the ugliness of their existence. Born in New York, where he studied at the Catholic University, he had his first big success as the handsome hustling waif in *Midnight Cowboy*, 1969. In both *Deliverance*, 1972, and *Coming Home*, 1978, he again inhabited the dark side of America: in the first, a back-to-nature weekend trip into the wilderness becomes a nightmare, in the second, he played a paraplegic Vietnam veteran. He has made few movies, tending to avoid pretty-boy roles for more interesting character parts. In 1979, however, he had a big tear-jerking success as an ex-boxer in *The Champ*.

ABOVE: publicity portrait for *Table for Five*, 1983

ROBERT DE NIRO

De Niro's predatory and sometimes overpowering masculinity frightens and compels so effectively because in it can be sensed the barely submerged rage and violence of a trapped man. As Travis Bickle, the deranged urban avenger in *Taxi Driver*, 1976, and as the metal-worker in *The Deer Hunter*, 1978, trying to come to terms with his terrible experiences in Vietnam, he was immediately identifiable with the victims of the age. An actor of huge range and extraordinary sexual magnetism, with the power to create in a film the sense of the hellish world in which his character exists, his characters seem emotionally behind their time, incapable of confronting their female side. In *New York, New York*, 1977, his dominating, self-centred chauvinist tells Liza Minnelli, 'You don't say goodbye to me, I say goodbye to you'.

But, for all their macho posturing, De Niro's males often end up as romantic losers; in *New York, New York*, Minnelli frees herself from his dominance to become a star and bring up their son alone, and in *The Last Tycoon*, 1976, De Niro's elegant studio boss, modelled on Irving Thalberg, was caught up in a hopeless, illusory love affair. Whether as the demented Johnny Boy of *Mean Streets*, 1973, the coolly graceful Vito Corleone of *The Godfather, Part II*, 1974, or the primitive Jake La Motta in *Raging Bull*, 1980, De Niro appears to live his roles, even changing physically. 'I can't cheat when I act,' he said, 'I know that the cinema is an illusion, but not for me.'

LEFT: publicity portrait for *The Deer Hunter*, 1978

DONALD SUTHERLAND

Attractively unwholesome, the Canadian-born Sutherland is one of the most interesting of leading men: he can be comic and disturbing at the same time, his expression turning in moments from protective warmth to a leer hinting at all kinds of repressed devilry. It is the kind of face that forty years ago would have put him straight into nasty roles, but in this day and age made him leading man of *Fellini's Casanova*, 1976.

It was Sutherland's aura of evil inanity that won him his first good part, as the psychopath in *The Dirty Dozen*, 1967, but his intriguing ambiguity, a blend of blank insubordination and authority, which turned him into a leading man in *M*A*S*H*, 1970, as the laid-back medic Hawkeye who fits in a round of golf amidst the mind-numbing gore. The next year, he found a very different, if still ambiguous, role in *Klute*, as a moral loner, a cop obsessed with finding a killer, who ropes in an unwilling hooker, Jane Fonda, to help him, then falls for her. Sutherland continued to play engaging weirdoes and ordinary men suffering from psychic disturbance; he was appalling as a trendy priest in *Little Murders*, 1971, but marvellous as the father who is persuaded to discard disbelief for a faith in the supernatural and the belief that his daughter is still alive in Roeg's thriller *Don't Look Now*, 1973. His perception of the undercurrents in apparent normality was reflected again in *Ordinary People*, 1980, in which he played the father of a traumatized family.

ABOVE: portrait, 1981

207

RYAN O'NEAL

WOODY ALLEN

Allen is a small, bespectacled, balding New Yorker who by conventional standards ought not to be a leading man. Nevertheless, he has directed and played leading man in three classic romantic films: *Annie Hall*, 1977, *Manhattan*, 1979, and *Stardust Memories*, 1980, opposite some very glamorous leading ladies.

Allen's heroes are all highly successful urban males who suffer from the same emotional masochism and fail to sustain relationships owing to their own obsessive insecurities. *Annie Hall* starts with the famous Groucho Marx joke that Allen would never belong to any club which would have him as a member; similarly, his need for love is always counterpointed by his mistrust of any women who would love someone like him.

BELOW: *Play It Again Sam*, 1972

The cherubic O'Neal had his first dose of international fame as the rebellious Rodney Harrington in 'Peyton Place', then found screen stardom as Oliver, the rich but nice college boy who falls in love with a poor but decent college girl, Ali MacGraw, in *Love Story*, 1970. Subsequently cast as a nice young man afflicted by unforeseen circumstances, he found three of his best roles in the seventies as the well-behaved musician transformed by scatty Barbra Streisand in the sprightly *What's Up Doc?*, then as the inept con-artist of *Paper Moon*, 1973, in which he was outstanding opposite his daughter Tatum, and finally as the getaway man in Walter Hill's brilliantly shot car chase movie *The Driver*, 1978. Off-screen, O'Neal lives with Farrah Fawcett.

ABOVE: publicity portrait for *The Driver*, 1978

JOHN TRAVOLTA

Without doubt, *Saturday Night Fever*, 1977, and *Grease*, 1978, made John Travolta the hottest movie property of the late seventies. Romantic looking in a raunchy Latin way, hip and streetwise, he had the works – teenage fans and a flourishing spin-off industry in posters, books, albums and magazines. But at present the adolescent passions he evoked seem to have been as ephemeral as those of the fifties for teen idols like Frankie Avalon and Troy Donahue, and it remains to be seen whether the mature Travolta can induce such fervour as he did when he was a pretty boy.

Born into a theatrical family, Travolta left school at sixteen to become an actor and worked hard for his success, both on television and the stage. He catapulted himself into big-screen stardom as a vulnerable, slightly lost street-hunk, first with disco dancing – for Hollywood it was an electric showing – then with some rather plastic rock-and-roll as Olivia Newton-John's gangleading sweetheart.

After *Grease*, Travolta tried to develop as an actor in *Moment by Moment*, 1978, playing a male prostitute in love with an older woman, Lily Tomlin, but the movie flopped badly; poignantly, his own girlfriend, actress Diana Hyland, who was seventeen years his senior, had died of cancer in 1977. Travolta retreated for two years, returning with moderate success in *Urban Cowboy*, but losing momentum again with *Staying Alive*, which was a poorly received spin-off of *Saturday Night Fever*.

RIGHT: publicity portrait for *Grease*, 1978

AL PACINO

Pacino's swarthy but sensitive features have a slightly baleful cast redeemed by the soulfulness of his eyes. His characters mirror this intriguing mixture of gentleness and violence, as in *The Godfather I* and *II*, Coppola's epic in which Pacino played Marlon Brando's avenging son, Michael Corleone, who matures from a taciturn war hero rejecting the Mafia code to the chillingly cold-blooded and isolated head of the family. He showed the same blend of aggression and tenderness in *Serpico*, as the cop with a hippy life-style in Greenwich Village who fights the system his own way, and in *Scarecrow*, 1973, in which he is Gene Hackman's violence-resisting partner who nearly gets beaten to death.

Born in a rough New York neighbourhood and of Sicilian descent, Pacino's parents separated when he was young; brought up by his mother and grandparents, he was rebellious and disturbed at school. He has an affinity for 'outsider' roles, conveying complex, stormy emotions with restraint; the impression is that Pacino has been there himself and doesn't want to talk about it too much. As such, there are elements in the persona that can be traced back to Bogart's defensive introspection in *Casablanca*, and to some of Eastwood's cool, austere, secretive heroes. Interestingly, in *Bobby Deerfield*, 1977, he plays a racing driver whose insecurities are literally hidden behind a defensive covering of helmet, dark glasses and racing overalls. His twitchy, inept bank robber whose crime was committed to finance his boyfriend's sex-change operation in *Dog Day Afternoon*, 1975, and cop hunting down a mass murderer in *Cruising*, 1980, both of whom explored the mores and psychology of sexual ambiguity.

LEFT: publicity portrait for *Scarecrow*, 1973

DUSTIN HOFFMAN

Hoffman is not very handsome, but he is extremely attractive. As a leading man, he is the sexy ingenu still discovering new delights: even now in his late forties, he retains the air of puzzled eroticism and youthful sense of adventure that made him a sex-symbol overnight in *The Graduate*, 1967. Held in thrall by Mrs Robinson, Anne Bancroft, and unable to fulfil his father's expectations, he achieved grace and a happy ending for the film by running off with Mrs Robinson's daughter as she stood at the altar with her awful fiancé her mother had approved for her.

Named after the silents star, Dustin Farnum, by his movie-mad mother,

Hoffman's character can be plotted from his mouth, which still curves up with an expression of gratified surprise, rather than down with the disillusionment of middle-age. It's this gentle quality which made him so ill-at-ease in the violence of *Straw Dogs*, a film which was far more up Pacino's street. Interestingly, several of his characters have involved him in the exploration of his female side: as the emasculated Ratso, mothering boyish, innocent Jon Voight in *Midnight Cowboy*, 1969, the father refusing Meryl Streep her son in *Kramer vs Kramer*, 1979, and the actor who becomes a woman for the sake of his

career, but resolves his personal dilemmas by reasserting his masculinity for love of Jessica Lange in *Tootsie*, 1982. What stops the Hoffman character from comic pathos is the seam of stubborn self-righteousness that lurks beneath his timid charm. He parodied it in the opening moments of *Tootsie*, when he justified to his agent his application of Method acting to the role of a tomato in a children's show.

ABOVE: *Agatha*, 1979

ROBERT REDFORD

ABOVE: *The Great Gatsby*, 1974, with Mia Farrow
OPPOSITE: publicity portrait for *The Sting*, 1973

Redford is a bafflingly ambivalent figure, his smile and eyes not quite co-ordinated in their message. On the one hand he can be the lovable, romping good buddy of *Butch Cassidy and the Sundance Kid* and *The Sting*, on the other, detached and honourable observer of the amoralities behind achievement and success – both his own and that of others. Riding along with him in the limousine in *The Candidate*, 1972, we are allowed to share in his disgusted self-knowledge as he intones his election address in tones of

perfect, resonant sincerity but sentences of pure gibberish. As 'Washington Post' investigative reporter Bob Woodward in *All the President's Men*, 1976, he is compelled by an internal sense of revulsion at the actions of others, which compels him to crack open the flawless façade of political lies and expose the emotional and moral defect beneath.

Although Redford's godlike handsomeness suggests all the Yuppie virtues – success, wealth, athletic achievement – he is in fact anti-urban

and honourable in intent, examining the pioneer spirit in *Jeremiah Johnson*, 1972, the treatment of the American Indian in *Tell Them Willie Boy is Here*, 1970, and the conflict of commercial values with ecological ones in *The Electric Horseman*, 1979.

Redford reached Hollywood through a roundabout route, dropping out of college to try out a career as a painter in Europe, then joining the American Academy of Dramatic Arts on his return. His first big screen success came in 1969, with *Butch Cassidy*, but he had been a leading man since taking his Broadway role in the romantic comedy 'Barefoot in the Park' to the screen in 1967.

His exploration of American attitudes to success and winning began in 1969 with *Downhill Racer*, in which he played an unlikable skier obsessed by his desire for a medal to the exclusion of all human requirements; there were similar elements in the aerial stuntman in *The Great Waldo Pepper*, 1975. In those kinds of role, his characters' emotional and sexual needs are negligible, their relationships negotiable, compared with their drive for power.

By the mid-seventies Redford was America's most popular box-office star. Avoiding off-screen publicity, Redford has a wife and three children, campaigns on environmental issues, esppuses liberal political causes and spends much of his time in Utah, of which he owns plenty — a ranch, a horse farm, a ski resort and several thousand acres of land.

ABOVE: publicity portrait for *The Way We Were*, 1973
RIGHT: *The Electric Horseman*, 1979, with Jane Fonda
OPPOSITE: publicity portrait for *The Natural*, 1984

NICK NOLTE

SYLVESTER STALLONE

Nolte is a rather vicious cherub, a huge, dimpled tough guy who is often an un-likely leading man. His role in *Teachers*, 1985, as a sympathetic teacher in a rough school, suggests he is developing the hard but dependable image of a modern Glenn Ford. He arrived in Hollywood in the late seventies through movies made for television, played opposite Jacqueline Bisset in *The Deep*, 1977, then found a more interesting role as the drug-running anti-hero in *Who'll Stop the Rain?*, 1978. His brawniest performance so far has been in the violent thriller *48 Hours*, 1982, as a San Francisco cop of few words – most of them foul – who springs Eddie Murphy from jail to help him nail the killers of two colleagues.

BELOW: publicity portrait for *Under Fire*, 1983

The success of *Rocky* in 1976 lifted Stallone from obscurity to top box-office draw and its two equally corny follow-ups have been far more suc-cessful than his ventures into other roles; as far as the public is concerned, Stallone is Rocky Balboa, the large, spaniel-eyed boxer with fairy-tale adventures which appear to parallel his own. Stallone claims he was down to his last few dollars when he saw a Muhammad Ali fight and was inspired to write *Rocky* which won the Oscar for Best Picture and made him a millionaire in only three days. As a child he was told by his father, 'You weren't born with much brain so you'd better develop your body', but his tough-guy aura is deceptive, and part of his appeal lies in his native cunning.

ABOVE: publicity portrait for *Rocky III*, 1982

RICHARD GERE

Richard Gere has a strutting sexual presence in some ways akin to that of Robert De Niro, but where De Niro is gawky, Gere is smooth; he smiles sleekly and sleepily and portrays rough, beautiful hulks from the wrong side of the tracks. Gere dropped out of university to act in rep, and worked on stage in London and on Broadway before moving off to Hollywood. Made a romantic-lead superstar by *An Officer and a Gentleman*, 1982, he had already bedded Diane Keaton in *Looking for Mr Goodbar*, 1977, and taken the lead in *Yanks* and *American Gigolo*, 1979. The latter clearly illustrates the changing role of the leading man; billed as 'the highest paid lover in Beverly Hills; he leaves women feeling more alive than they've ever felt before', Gere played a narcissistic male prostitute framed for the murder of a client. Interestingly, rather than spoil his new romantic image, the film did better at the box-office, subsequent to the success of *An Officer and a Gentleman*. He is lately to be seen in the highly expensive *The Cotton Club*, playing a white jazz musician.

RIGHT: publicity portrait for *American Gigolo*, 1979

GERARD DEPARDIEU

Depardieu calls to mind both Jean Gabin and Jean-Paul Belmondo. Since *Les Valseuses*, 1974, in which he established his rugged, working-class image as a virile petty criminal, he has become one of the biggest sex symbols in European cinema and his status was confirmed when he co-starred with Robert De Niro in *1900*, as a peasant turned partisan-hero.

Depardieu's role in *Les Valseuses* is said to contain many elements of his own childhood. He became attracted to acting while working as a beach-boy in Cannes during the Film Festival, went to Paris to train, then worked his way up through television and the theatre. A forceful presence, Depardieu has often been an off-beat leading man, presented several times as the object of female subversion and rage. In *The Last Woman*, he castrated himself with an electric knife, in *Bye Bye Monkey* he was raped by a feminist theatre group in a ghastly New York some time in the future, and struggled with bewilderment to conquer his girl's depressions only for her to abandon him in favour of a pubescent boy in *Préparez Vos Mouchoirs*. In *The Return of Martin Guerre*, he played the part of a medieval peasant who leaves his village as a callow newly-wed, only to return years later as a supposed war-hero. Welcomed with open arms by the village, his identity is later challenged and he is sentenced to death by the ecclesiastical court, but only after his wife has knowingly abandoned the law, and truth, to plead for him through her love.

ABOVE: *1900*, 1976

218

CHRISTOPHER REEVE

WILLIAM HURT

In a Hollywood which has been dominated by ethnic heroes, such as Pacino and Hoffman, and all-American hunks like Reeve and Ford, Hurt has been seen as 'the great white hope of American acting'. Of all the stars now emerging, he seems the most capable of providing sophisticated passion for the post-feminist woman. In *Body Heat*, 1982, a steamy reworking of *Double Indemnity*, he plays a struggling young lawyer seduced into murder by a beautiful woman, and in *Gorky Park*, 1983, the honest Moscow cop faced with a gruesome triple murder to solve.

BELOW: publicity portrait for *Body Heat*, 1982

Reeve as Superman represents the male of both the seventies and eighties. Clark Kent, the bumbling, bespectacled, earthbound mortal, belongs to the seventies as a leading man with problems asserting his masculinity in a feminist age; while Superman, his macho alter-ego in blue tights, who can repair countries and pull cars out of a rock-fall, reveals the powerful accentuated torso and shoulders which represent today's sexually self-confident man.

With *Superman* behind him, Reeve is developing into a creditable actor, most notably opposite Michael Caine in *Death Trap*, 1982, and as Basil Ransome in the film of Henry James's novel, *The Bostonians*.

ABOVE: publicity portrait for *Death Trap*, 1982

MEL GIBSON

Mel Gibson had his first big film success with *Tim*, 1979, for which he won the Australian Film Award for Best Actor, and achieved international renown as one of the innocents in *Gallipoli*. Tough and truculently sexy, an intriguing slight twitchiness about his mouth and with a spunky all-Australian image — although he was born in New York — he started to develop a cult persona along the lines of a Clint Eastwood anti-hero, in *Mad Max 1* and *2*. More recently he took off on a completely different track in *The Year of Living Dangerously*, in which he had some steamy scenes opposite Sigourney Weaver. In 1984 he played Fletcher Christian in *The Bounty*.

ABOVE: publicity portrait for *The Bounty*, 1984

HARRISON FORD

Ford's mild demeanour and almost lethargic delivery, as though speaking with a cigarette clenched between his teeth, belies his resourcefulness, expediency and practicality as a fantasy hero and rebellious good guy. Masculine in a comfortable way, his lazy grace can be better appreciated in middle-shots than close-ups. Ford's best film so far has been *Raiders of the Lost Ark*, 1981, as the tongue-in-cheek archaeologist who, like his other heroes, falls for a good-looking, pragmatic girl in the course of multiple adventures. His career only began to move after *American Graffiti*, 1973. Following *Star Wars*, 1977, he has found more challenging roles in *Blade Runner*, 1982, and *Witness*, 1985.

BELOW: *Raiders of the Lost Ark*, 1981

JEREMY IRONS

Jeremy Irons's international stardom is evidence of the hardiness of the sensitive upper-class Englishman, as portrayed in the thirties by Leslie Howard. Irons worked as a social worker and a busker in London's West End before training at drama school in Bristol, and got his first break as Judas in 'Godspell', then rocketed to heart-throb fame in the television series 'Brideshead Revisited', which was based on Evelyn Waugh's classic novel, but filmed as a British aristo-cratic version of the male buddy story. He achieved international stardom opposite Meryl Streep in *The French Lieutenant's Woman* as a Victorian gentleman who begins an affair with a lady's companion in a seaside town.

His screen image contains a certain ambiguity and weakness. Elegant and frail, he declared his passion for Patricia Hodge in *Betrayal* with a string of fine phrases in a beautifully fur-nished bedroom, but his affair with Hodge was complicated by the fact that she was married to his best friend, publisher, Ben Kingsley; a very British concept of males loyally uniting against woman the foe. His slightly obsessed, haunted look also made him a good choice for the nervous Polish foreman in *Moonlighting*.

RIGHT: portrait, 1983

MATT DILLON

SAM SHEPARD

Sam Shepard was recently described as 'the American West's version of Renaissance man'. In 1984, he stole the show in *The Right Stuff* as heroic test pilot Chuck Yeager, and the film he wrote for director Wim Wenders, *Paris Texas*, won the 'Palme d'Or' at the Cannes Film Festival. Meanwhile, his play 'Fool for Love' opened in London and New York.

Both as a leading man and writer, his work is strongly concerned with the fragmentation, violence and unhappiness of society – what he once called 'the macho psyche of the American male', as personified by Clint Eastwood and Charles Bronson – and the hero ethic. 'It's an American tradition. We make heroes all the time.' He lives with actress Jessica Lange, whom he appeared with in *Frances*, 1982.

BELOW: publicity portrait for *Frances*, 1982

Spotted prowling the corridors of his high school by casting agent Vic Ramos, who was impressed by Dillon's streetwise charisma – although he in fact hails from a middle-class family background – Dillon has the brooding, raw-boned features and the wolf-like grace the camera loves. He has been carefully groomed by Ramos as the James Dean of the eighties; his first film, *Over the Edge*, was standard *Rebel without a Cause* stuff, and in his second film, *Little Darlings*, 1980, he played sex object to Tatum O'Neal and Kristy McNichol so steamily that he received a thousand fan letters a day. Films like *Rumble Fish* and *The Outsiders*, both 1983, have developed the image of the kid from the wrong side of the tracks.

ABOVE: publicity portrait for *Rumble Fish*, 1983

Penn is one of few distinctive screen males of the eighties; neat, clean-cut and strong jawed, but with a pair of close-set eyes that add to his air of overt sexual threat. He made his screen debut in the Barnaby Jones television series in 1979, but his first important screen role was as the clean-cut student at the military academy in *Taps*.

The Californian-born Penn boasts two parents in showbiz – his mother was an actress, his father a television director – and he made home movies at high school before working on stage and off with the Los Angeles Group Repertory Theatre. He has recently graduated to some interesting roles in films like *Racing with the Moon*, opposite Elizabeth McGovern, Louis Malle's caper movie *Crackers*, in which he starred with Donald Sutherland, and John Schlesinger's *The Falcon and The Snowman*, opposite Timothy Hutton.

RIGHT: *Racing With The Moon*, 1984

INDEX